John R. Hosfield

Love

Georgia

Classic Country Inns of America

New England and The Maritimes

To: John and Bill,
Merry Christmas ('79)
and our love alway,
    Georgia and Jon

CLASSIC COUNTRY INNS OF AMERICA
VOLUME I

Inns of New England and The Maritimes

BY PETER ANDREWS

PHOTOGRAPHED BY LILO RAYMOND

AN ARCHITECTURAL DIGEST BOOK

THE
KNAPP PRESS
LOS ANGELES

HOLT,
RINEHART
AND WINSTON
NEW YORK

Library of Congress Cataloging in Publication Data

Andrews, Peter, 1931–
    Inns of New England and the Maritimes.

    (His Classic country inns of America; v. 1)
    1. Hotels, taverns, etc.—New England.
2. Hotels, taverns, etc.—Canada—Maritime Provinces.
I. Raymond, Lilo, joint author. II. Title.
III. Series.
TX909.A58   647'.9474   77-71352
ISBN 0-03-042836-X

First Edition
Printed in the United States of America

10 9 8 7 6 5 4 3 2 1

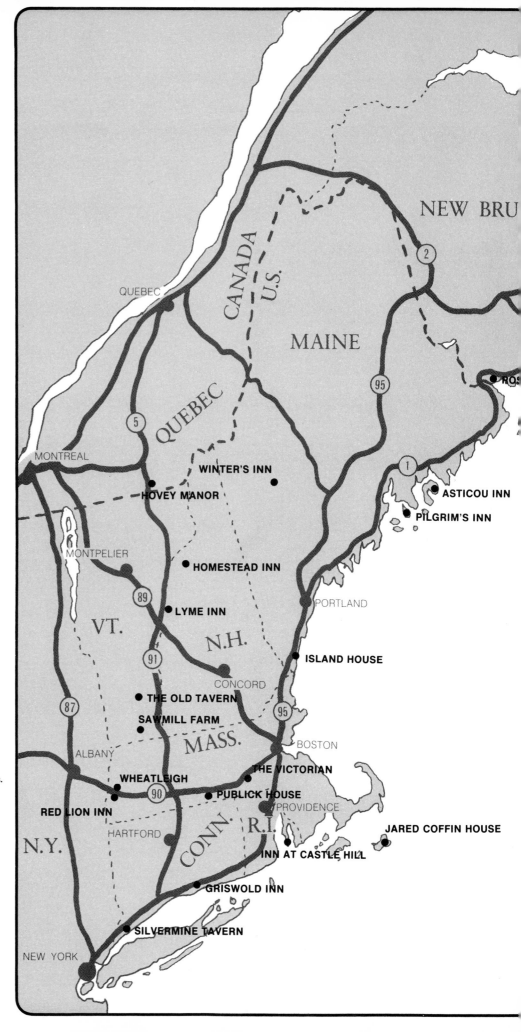

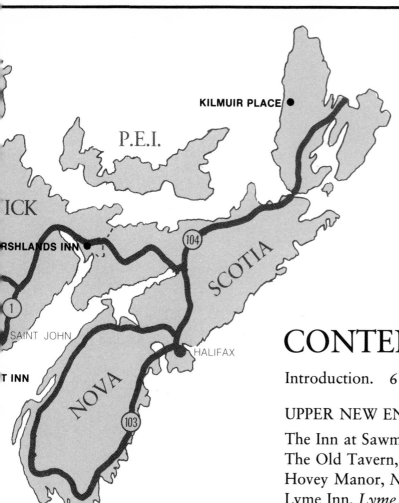

CONTENTS

* Photographed by George Gardner

Michael Thom
Winter's Inn

THE SPIRIT OF INNKEEPING

The nature of the country inn in North America has changed considerably in the last two hundred years. During colonial times, inns, or taverns as they were then called, were at the very center of community activity. Farmers came by to talk about the weather and merchants conducted business in the taproom. The tavernkeeper was often one of the leading citizens of the town. It was he who greeted visitors and diligently inquired about events in other portions of the colonies. As the break with England approached, taverns and inns were the places where patriots met to plot a little treason against the Monarch.

In the early days of the nation, taverns sprang up as new communities were founded. An establishment like the Old Tavern in Grafton, Vermont, was just what a growing town needed: people new to the community could stay there until they got settled; agents from the growing cities put up there when dealing with local manufacturers.

Around the 1850s, railroads made a big difference to American traveling patterns, and railroad hotels, built near the stations in every community of any size, soon usurped the old functions of the local inn and tavern. The inns had to find a new focus, and they did, as the hectic life of the cities and the writers of the time made the idea of a retreat to the country appealing. Longfellow romanticized the experience in his *Tales of a Wayside Inn,* and Emerson spoke of the restorative effects of a trip to the mountains. The Homestead, a New Hampshire inn, was started in the 1880s by a farm family who felt the vacationer's desire for good food and a little peace in an inspiring landscape.

As the age of the automobile approached, by the 1930s, the clientele became a bit fickle. With a car one might go anywhere, and this new freedom, with its delight in distances traveled rather than destinations achieved, sent America's inns into a severe decline. First roadside cabins, then motels, serviced the newly independent travelers, to the point where only a lucky few of the inns of an earlier day were able to survive.

As Americans sped toward the space age, though, they began to

Paul McEnroe
The Inn at Castle Hill

7

Florence Brooks-Dunay
and David Weisgal
Wheatleigh

George and Eleanor Pavloff,
with their daughter Elena
Pilgrim's Inn

William Winterer
Griswold Inn

rediscover the rich heritage of these charming spots. It is safe to say that in the last thirty years more work has gone into restoring and preserving America's heritage of country inns than went into their original construction. Additionally, an imaginative new breed of inn-keepers has remodeled barns, grist mills, private homes and hotels into country inns that reflect and recapture the spirit of hospitality that characterized earlier times.

It is easy to see why today's travelers are flocking to these marvelous inns. They have a style and a sense of time and place that modern hotels cannot match. But why would any sane person want to run one? It certainly cannot be just for the money. A last-minute cancellation at the Waldorf-Astoria is a minor inconvenience to the management, but to an innkeeper with only six rooms to let, it can mean the difference between profit and loss for the week. Yet there seems to be some primordial satisfaction in creating a safe haven for travelers. As Rodney

Fred and Judy Siemons
Lyme Inn

Williams, who left a successful architectural practice to create the Inn at Sawmill Farm, says, "I am earning half the income I used to but I am enjoying life twice as much."

Modern innkeepers are a diverse lot. Some have been trained professionally, like Francis Whitman, Jr., of the Silvermine Tavern, who attended the famous Cornell school of hotel management. Guests in the house have always been part of Esther Serafini's life. She learned the business by working in her family's inn, the Homestead, from the time she was eight years old. For many, however, innkeeping is a second start in life. Paul McEnroe, who now operates the Inn at Castle Hill in Newport, was a successful real estate and insurance broker when he was bitten by the inn bug. He found he took inordinate pleasure in being a host.

Other new innkeepers have the same feeling. Used to having servants in his old home, David Weisgal abandoned a career in estate management to run the majestic Wheatleigh in the Berkshires. Now he sleeps

Esther Tefft Serafini
The Homestead

Isabel Taylor
Kilmuir Place

George and Marion Brewin
Rossmount Inn

in the servants' quarters, does most of the heavy work around the inn, and loves every minute of it. "I'm on stage all the time," he says. "I'm the lord of the manor."

Good innkeeping requires a deft, personal touch. Innkeeper George Brewin, of Rossmount Inn, is the only waiter in the dining room every night, sometimes serving not only the guests staying in his twenty rooms upstairs, but the public as well. Yet he manages to make each diner feel important.

Most inns, no matter how informal, have rituals, as well. When guests leave the Homestead, they are given a New Hampshire serenade as they go. Esther Serafini, and as many of her staff as can make it, rush to the front of the house, pick up bells from the collection in the hall, and stand on the porch shaking them for all they're worth. Sleigh bells, cow bells, dinner bells, all kinds of bells. It is the merry sound of gracious innkeeping that makes people want to come back again and again.

Ione and Rodney Williams
The Inn at Sawmill Farm

Philip and Margaret Read
Jared Coffin House

THE INN
AT SAWMILL FARM

West Dover, Vermont

Comforts and pleasures.

Sawmill Farm's swimming pool stands just above the farmhouse, which contains a splendid suite of rooms. The view from the pool to the town below, shown above, reveals the new tennis court as well. The Williamses put it in not only for guests, but for themselves; they are avid players.

When Rodney and Ione Williams decided to remodel a farm on the site of an eighteenth-century sawmill and convert it into an inn, they brought up a silver birch tree from their old home in New Jersey and planted it on their new property. Bringing a birch tree to a state that is already famous for them must have seemed strange to the people in the area, but Rod and Ione knew what they were doing. The tree now grows up through an enclosure within the house, a natural touch amid the elegance that marks the Inn at Sawmill Farm. Rod is an architect; Ione, a professional decorator. Together they have created a country inn filled with stunning effects, both indoors and out.

Simply driving up to the inn is an aesthetic experience. The smell of apple trees is in the air, and the house is surrounded by slate walks, gravel patios and meandering rock gardens. There is a rose garden, too, a rarity for Vermont. The entrance hall inside establishes a dramatic mood. Barn siding is used with such abandon as an interior decoration that it becomes as luxurious as the finest paneling. Farm implements are hung on the wall next to a gargantuan window that opens out to the vistas beyond. Carved out of an ell in the old barn, the main living room is a vast space with exposed beams showing off its original post-and-brace structure. The room is highlighted by an oversized fireplace surrounded by the Williamses' collection of copper utensils. To the west, the wall is all windows, but the afternoon light is screened by the majestic old trees outside. A balcony area above the living room, in the old hayloft, houses a library.

Rod's architectural instinct is for a feeling of movement. In most

New England country inns, each room seems self-contained, but, at Sawmill, every space leads on to the next. The inn's main dining room can be glimpsed beyond the living room. With a twenty-foot ceiling soaring high above the Queen Anne-style chairs, it is a formal room, elegantly proportioned. In the summer, each table displays a fresh lily from the garden, and wood-bladed fans paddle overhead when the weather is warm. The dining room opens to the low-ceilinged, small, but social Pot Belly Bar. Paneled in barn siding and hung with paintings, the bar contains the Williamses' collection of copper kettles, ancient ice skates, biscuit tins and a player piano that can play anything from *Beer Barrel Polka* to Sigmund Romberg. By enclosing a porch beyond the bar, Rod has created a pair of intimate dining rooms that contain a small greenhouse where bougainvillea climbs up over the white-painted beamed ceiling.

The bedroom accommodations, ranging from single and double rooms to two-bedroom suites with fireplaces, are all deluxe. Each room has been given its own distinctive style. Some are Victorian and some reflect the New England country style. Still others have been done

Fabulous food.

The food at the inn is based on the freshest possible ingredients prepared with precision and ingenuity. The settings in which it is served include a formal room in the old barn, opposite, and a glass-walled bower overlooking the swimming pool, left. Red snapper is shown cooked and uncooked, although the latter isn't on the menu. The roast duck is, however.

16

in a more formal colonial mode and are furnished in exquisite Chippendale.

Ione once did almost all the cooking, and she still bakes the pies. She has found a brilliant chef to take over the workload, though, in the unlikely person of her son Brill. Trained as an electrical engineer, Brill, now in his late twenties, decided not to pursue that career and came up to Vermont to work at Sawmill Farm. As they remodeled, he learned carpentry and stonemasonry. Most importantly, however, he found he had a natural talent for the kitchen. With Brill leading the way, the whole Williams family has a hand in the preparation of the meals at the inn. Their aim is fine dining, a meal that is an experience in itself. Guests usually find themselves dining the full two hours that Escoffier says is the proper amount of time to devote to a meal.

Brill runs a busy kitchen. As at most country inns, much of the food, especially the vegetables, is locally grown; however, Brill also orders up fish and meat from Boston, produce from Albany, duckling from Long Island and has fresh crab flown up from Maryland.

No inn is ever static, but the Inn at Sawmill Farm is an unusually active place behind the scenes. Rod and Ione are constantly making improvements and additions. Under their direction, the inn is growing to fulfill their vision of the perfect country inn. They put in a swimming pool early on, and recently installed a large, new kitchen for Brill to work in. Rod is putting in dormer windows to give the hayloft bedrooms more light, and Ione is making preparations for a stone and brick wine cellar. To guests, however, the atmosphere is peaceful and calm.

A separate peace.

The fireplace of the living room in the old barn shelters a plant in summer, left. The inn offers guest accommodations in several buildings. The downstairs suite at the cider house, below left, has a rustic appeal, and a hammock next to the trout pond is the perfect place to spend an afternoon.

19

An inside look.

At left is the porch railing of the inn's farmhouse. At right, above, is the great window of the entrance hall. The bedroom above and the living room, far right above, are striking examples of Ione's decorating genius. Tartans and chintzes are an impossible combination, but here they work. Suites in the spring house, above, are shaded by old apple trees.

Rod and Ione are always doing something extra for their guests. Christmas is a special time at the inn and the Williamses put on their own holiday celebration for those who come up to try their skills on nearby Mount Snow. On Christmas Eve, they serve a huge holiday feast of roast beef and Yorkshire pudding, and then everyone troops down to the church in town for the midnight service. Afterward, it's back to the inn for carols around the tree. Christmas Day begins with a special breakfast of crêpes stuffed with apples and topped with smoked Vermont ham simmered in maple syrup. Then the Williamses arrange some kind of special outing. One year, they organized a cross-country ski excursion. Rod and Brill pretended to get lost, and, while ostensibly leading the group back to the inn, they led them instead to a huge banquet laid out and waiting for them in the middle of the forest, with champagne chilling in the snow.

"It was the sort of thing," said one guest, "that makes the inn perfect for special occasions. It would be torture to live so well and eat so well all of the time, but they do make you wish such special occasions came more often."

THE OLD TAVERN

Grafton, Vermont

 Grafton, Vermont, pristine and perfect with its immaculate houses and graceful elms, seems to be an artist's idealized version of a classic nineteenth-century New England village, which is exactly what it is. A remarkable historic preservation effort by a group of private citizens known as the Windham Foundation has ensured Grafton's future by taking it back into the past. As a result, Grafton is now not a re-creation of what the community was 150 years ago, but the fulfillment of what it wanted to be.

The centerpiece of the restoration is the Old Tavern. Built in 1801, it was the social center of the area and sometimes doubled as the local courthouse. It knew its first real glory when a pair of Grafton brothers, Harlan and Francis Phelps, bought the place in 1865. Harlan brought his entire stake from eight years of prospecting during the California gold rush, $4,800, to pay for needed additions. Francis brought boundless energy and imagination. Stage driver, raconteur and genial host, Francis was the animating spirit of the inn. He organized the Grafton Cornet Band, which still plays on the village green, and made the tavern into a favorite haunt for the celebrities of the day. General Ulysses S. Grant was a guest at Christmas in 1867. The Old Tavern was much enjoyed by the Boston literary set, and such authors as Henry David Thoreau, Nathaniel Hawthorne, Ralph Waldo Emerson and Oliver Wendell Holmes, Sr., were frequent visitors. When Rudyard Kipling married American Caroline Balestier, in 1892, the couple honeymooned at the tavern.

The changing lifestyles of the twentieth century, as automobiles and motels took the place of coaches and wayside resting places, were hard on many New England communities, particularly towns such as Grafton

Vermont classic.

The Old Tavern's pillared porch came about when a longer and wider third floor was placed above the earlier brick structure. Summer rockers, something of a symbol for taking one's ease, are found on both the upstairs and downstairs porches.

A firm foundation.

A portrait of Dean Mathey, major benefactor of the Windham Foundation, hangs in an Old Tavern room that duplicates his study in Princeton, New Jersey.

25

The charm of objects.

The inn displays a fascinating range of collections. Decoys are on display in the Pine Dining Room. The sign in the Homestead cottage barn is one of many. Beautiful, individual Chippendale and Windsor chairs are placed throughout the public rooms.

that relied heavily on transient trade. In 1963, there was not a single shop or store in Grafton, and the tavern was open only during the summer season and was losing money even then. Happily, the Windham Foundation stepped in that year and undertook a revitalization of the tavern and of the surrounding community.

The tavern has been meticulously restored. The foundation has filled the rooms with a profusion of antiques. There is a rich variety of panelings brought from nineteenth-century buildings in Vermont and New Hampshire. On the walls are a number of charming period paintings and prints, including superb examples of formal New England portraiture. The floors are laid with clear, wide pine boards and finished in the golden hue of melted butter. Everything about the reconstruction shows the traditional Yankee respect for good materials and superior craftsmanship. The taproom, located in the original barn, is paneled with antique boards and traversed by a huge beam salvaged from a bridge in northern Vermont.

The tavern has the air of a small but select New England college. In the downstairs recreation rooms, instructive sayings of some of the tavern's famous guests are painted on the walls: "Character is a by-product. It is produced in the manufacture of daily duty"—Woodrow Wilson; and "Treat them like men, but remember they are just boys"—Frank Boyden, legendary headmaster of Deerfield Academy. With all this rectitude in evidence, the bedrooms are surprisingly rich and

26

Collegiate connection.

The hallway between the Homestead and Windham cottages, with its painted wainscoting and bull's-eye glass, shows the Neo-Georgian restraint of buildings at many New England colleges.

Colonial romantic.

Fringed bedspreads, low, comfortable boudoir chairs and hooked rugs in old designs contribute to the mood of the inn's bedrooms.

romantic. Several feature exceptional crewel work or brocade, and many have canopied beds and fireplaces. Antique mirrors reflect rooms appointed with fringed draperies, lush chaises and flowered wallpaper. Some of the most pleasant accommodations offered by the tavern are in the Homestead and Windham cottages across the street. The sunny corridor that connects the two cottages is a perfect place to dawdle or perhaps read a novel plucked from the glass-encased antique bookcase in the hall.

Food at the tavern is hearty and plentiful. Breakfast is served in the loggia facing the neatly laid-out croquet lawn, where a folk art figure of an early Grafton settler stands amid a flowered border. Dinner is served either in the Chippendale main room, formally hung with Georgian chandeliers, or in the heavy-beamed, denlike Pine Room.

The Old Tavern is in the heart of the Vermont resort area. In the summer, tennis courts are available right on the property, and there is excellent golf on three nearby courses. The Old Tavern also boasts a proper New England swimming hole that recalls the days when Thoreau loved his bracing dips in forest ponds. In the winter, skiers staying at the Old Tavern are guaranteed reservations on the slopes of Timber Ridge. But guests don't have to go very far afield if they don't want to. The tavern will pack picnic lunches for those who choose to explore the many walking trails in the area. The town of Grafton is also a charming place for a stroll. The old cheese-making industry has been revived, and once again cheddar cheese from Grafton is being sold coast to coast. No nineteenth-century New England town would be complete without a blacksmith's shop, and the one in Grafton, right next to the livery stable, is maintained exactly as Hank Farnsworth kept it many years ago.

Although there is still work to be done, the Old Tavern and the community of Grafton are more than fulfilling the Windham Foundation's motto, *Floreat florebit,* "It flourished in the past, it will flourish in the future."

27

HOVEY MANOR

North Hatley, Quebec

Hovey Manor, in the green mountains of Canada, represents the dream of a pair of adventurous men who lived more than 150 years apart. In 1793, one Captain Ebenezer Hovey of Windsor, Connecticut, who had remained loyal to the crown following the American Revolution, struck out for the Canadian wilds to found a new settlement. Less than 50 miles beyond the Vermont border, Captain Hovey discovered glistening Lake Massawippi in the heart of the Quebec mountains. Game was plentiful and the lakes teemed with trout, salmon, bass and perch. The area had everything Hovey was looking for, so he decided to sink his roots in this mountain retreat and in 1803 he became the first settler of Hatley Township.

A century and a half later, a man with a different kind of dream came to the lake. His name was Bob Brown and he was an experienced hotel man. He had trained at the world-famous School of Hotel Administration at Cornell University and had worked for the Cardy Corporation, a privately owned chain in Canada. But when the Cardy hotels were swallowed up by a giant international complex, Brown decided to quit and go out on his own. One of Brown's favorite quotations is from Dr. Samuel Johnson, who said, "There is nothing which has yet been contrived by man by which so much happiness is produced as by a good inn or tavern."

Brown wanted to be an innkeeper and he found his chance in a sprawling colonial mansion on the west bank of Lake Massawippi. The house had been built in 1900 by a transplanted Georgian named Henry Atkinson who had erected an almost exact replica of George Washington's Mount Vernon home south of Alexandria, Virginia. The mansion overlooking the lake, with its gracious white columns, was

Steaks rare.

The chefs at Hovey Manor's Saturday night barbecue focus intensely on the fire, where the bounty of the inn is in preparation. The huge fireplace in the manor's Tap Room, shown above also, evokes reminiscences of Gargantua.

A separate space.
This cozy corner under the stairs contains the only telephone for guests at the inn. The old iron stove near the main staircase is an interesting remnant of former days, even though it no longer works.

just what Brown had been searching for. He bought the place in 1950 and immediately began converting it into one of the most impressive country inns in North America.

The conversion went slowly at the start. There was no foundation under the mansion and no heating inside it. During its first full year of operation Hovey Manor was able to accommodate only twenty guests for two months during the middle of the summer. Today, Hovey Manor is a busy year-round resort with upwards of one hundred overnight guests at any one time.

"Hospitality," said Ralph Waldo Emerson, who appreciated comfort *and* privacy, "consists of a little fire, a little food and an immense quiet." Hovey Manor offers this kind of quiet refuge for those guests who seek it. Eight cottages, originally ice and pump houses, ring the thirty acres of the estate and provide perfect seclusion for visitors and honeymooners who want to be quietly alone.

The main building at Hovey Manor is constantly buzzing with the myriad of activities that are associated with a major resort. Hefty

Northern skies, southern light.
Above the lake, the precincts of Hovey Manor gleam in spring sunlight. The pictures at right are from the capacious main building. The shop sign, bottom near right, is one of a number in the resort town of North Hatley.

LA ROSE DES VENTS

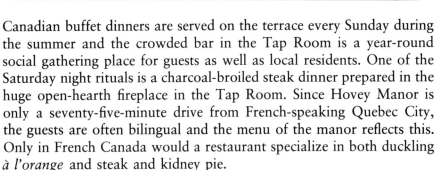

Canadian buffet dinners are served on the terrace every Sunday during the summer and the crowded bar in the Tap Room is a year-round social gathering place for guests as well as local residents. One of the Saturday night rituals is a charcoal-broiled steak dinner prepared in the huge open-hearth fireplace in the Tap Room. Since Hovey Manor is only a seventy-five-minute drive from French-speaking Quebec City, the guests are often bilingual and the menu of the manor reflects this. Only in French Canada would a restaurant specialize in both duckling *à l'orange* and steak and kidney pie.

In addition to conference facilities for business groups from five to fifty, Hovey Manor offers individual guests unusually gracious private accommodations. Each room has its own bath and many of them have wood-burning fireplaces. The manor is a treasure house of Canadian antiques, particularly that enchanting style known as French Primitive, which took good, sensible country furniture and gave it a touch of Gallic sophistication.

The emphasis at Hovey Manor is on the outdoor life because the mountains around Lake Massawippi are a sportsman's paradise. For fishermen, the lake yields up no less than forty-two varieties of fish including bass, salmon and three different kinds of trout. The manor has its own facilities for tennis and that Canadian passion, badminton. There are eight championship golf courses within a half hour's drive.

In the winter, the whole area turns into ski country with what aficionados claim is the deepest and whitest snow anywhere in the East. Hovey Manor is strategically located near six major slopes, including the impressive Canadian runs at Mount Orford, Mount Sutton and Bromont, as well as Vermont's Owl's Head and Jay Peak. Through an agreement with other resorts in the area, guests at Hovey Manor can get an interchangeable ticket to ski on one or all of these slopes. When Massawippi is frozen over, it becomes a perfect place for snowshoeing and cross-country skiing. More sedentary guests can amuse themselves by punching a hole in the ice and fishing or just enjoy themselves sitting out on the terrace at sundown, watching the migratory flight of a flock of snow geese overhead, although they may wonder why any creatures would want to leave this delightful mountain setting.

32

Mr. Brown's plantation.

Lake Massawippi is a central element of Hovey Manor's landscape. It lies at the foot of the hill, a pleasant prospect for guests relaxing on the porch or in chairs on the lawn. A fence characteristic of the American South runs along the road at the entrance to the grounds, right.

34

LYME INN

Lyme, New Hampshire

The Lyme Inn has undergone a number of transformations on its way to becoming one of the showplaces of New England. Built in 1809, it was first known as the Grant Hotel, and quickly became the social center of Lyme, New Hampshire, although not always with the approval of some of the more conservative elements in the community. "Dances are held Tuesday evenings in Grant's Hall," Mary Washburn noted crisply in her diary in 1869. "The Christian Community cannot but regret that dancing is regularly supported."

35

The hotel ceased operation in 1870, and was subsequently turned into an apartment building. During the late nineteenth century, the old place also saw service as a millinery shop and a Grange meeting hall. Around 1918, it was turned back into a tavern, which operated until shortly before the outbreak of World War II. The building then changed hands frequently, becoming a little shabbier with each new owner, until 1949, when the Gordon Cravens took the place over and began restoring some of its nineteenth-century character.

The restoration was brought to a happy conclusion by Ray and Connie Bergendoff, who bought the Lyme Inn in 1970. Under their direction, the inn became what it is now, an extraordinary melding of old-world charm and modern-day efficiency. Connie is an antiques dealer with a keen eye, and she filled the place with pieces from all over New England, making the Lyme Inn an informal museum of nineteenth-century American art and artifacts. Works by Currier and Ives and many of their contemporaries are on vivid display, along with a handsome collection of early New Hampshire maps, and a sampling of richly romantic prints from the days when the men all looked like Lord Byron, and the ladies swooned for their loved ones. The collection

Town pride.

At Lyme Lake, fall brings vivid color to a rocky bank. At the inn, above, falling leaves reveal a gray-green facade. A papier mâché milliner's dummy, inset, sits on a painted chest inside, where rooms were once used as a milliner's shop.

of artifacts includes antique spinning wheels, a large selection of cast-iron doorstops and colorful throw pillows created by local artisans. The Lyme Inn is as much an antiques store as it is an inn. Almost all of the furnishings and art objects are for sale to discerning collectors.

In 1976, Fred Siemons, a New Jersey food service manager, and his wife Judy, a registered nurse, decided they wanted to become New England innkeepers. They had been to the Lyme Inn before, and, like most of its guests, had succumbed to its sturdy charm. In looking for a place of their own, they made the Lyme Inn their standard of excellence. They were delighted to find that the inn was available. They bought it the following year, and took over active management in the summer of 1977.

Fred and Judy are thoroughly sympathetic to what the Bergendoffs have done. Judy has commissioned local artisans to make quilts for the beds that lacked them. Accustomed to work behind the scenes, Fred has smoothly slipped into Ray Bergendoff's role as genial host in the bar and dining room.

Not all guest rooms have their own baths, but the bedrooms are delightful. One of the most interesting is the Strawberry Room, where everything—wallpaper, art work, furnishings and bedspread—has some kind of strawberry motif. There is even a little basket of cloth strawberries on the mirrored Victorian chest, which is also painted with strawberry designs.

Downstairs, the setting is quietly nineteenth-century, with stenciled

Common sense.

The sun porch provides a prospect of Lyme Common, on which the inn and town church are the principal public buildings. Although the inn itself is right on the common, many of its windows, like the one at right, look out on forested slopes and woods.

wallpaper, plenty of wing chairs, a pressed tin ceiling and wicker furniture on the spacious front sun porch. There is only one television set in the entire building, and that is nicely tucked away in a sitting room. There is also a good selection of books and guests who get caught up in a volume are permitted to take it home with them as long as they send it back when they have finished.

As with many such New England establishments, the Lyme Inn is really two facilities under a single roof: a quiet refuge for overnight guests and a busy meeting place for the people who live in the area. The Lyme Inn is a favorite place for alumni and members of the faculty of Dartmouth ten miles up the road. No place can be quiet when there are a lot of Dartmouth men around, and particularly on a big game weekend, the Lyme Inn takes on a collegiate air.

The area is famous for its winter sports activities. Near the inn there is ice skating on a pond that is lit up at night, and demanding alpine skiing is available three miles away at the Dartmouth Skiway. There are five major ski areas within an hour's drive from the inn, and several cross-country and snowshoe trails in between. But Lyme has become a year-round resort area. As Fred Siemons says, "The beauty of the countryside in the winter is striking. It's peaceful in the summer, but in fall, when the foliage attracts visitors from all over, it overwhelms us every time."

Bedding down.

Antique bedsteads in great variety fill the inn's rooms. The third floor bedrooms were once the ballroom. The red plastic braided rug in the bathroom above is a good-humored send-up of the inn's carefully-finished antique decor. The strawberry wallpaper mentioned in the text is shown in the small bedroom photo.

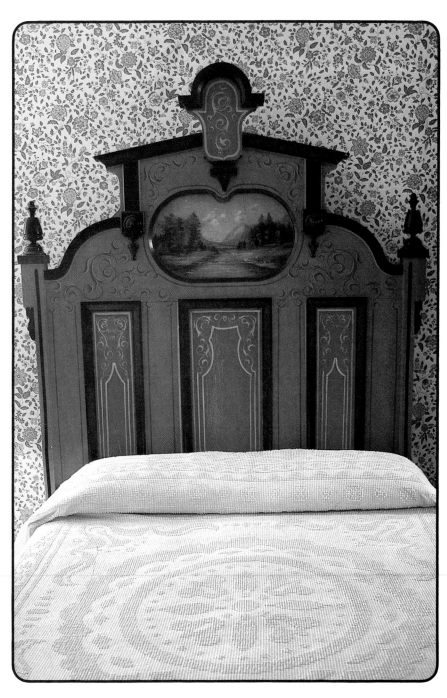

39

40

THE HOMESTEAD

Sugar Hill, New Hampshire

The first permanent settler in Sugar Hill, New Hampshire, was Moses Aldrich, who came upon this hillside country in 1780, bringing with him only a packhorse and a few rough tools. He cleared off a single, stony acre, planted a bushel of wheat to establish his claim and began to work the land. The 1780s were tough times for New England farmers. In Massachusetts, the situation became so desperate for bankrupt farmers that they took up arms in the ill-fated Shays' Rebellion of 1786–87 that, for a time, threatened to destroy the fragile new republic. But New Hampshire men have always been a hardy breed, and Moses Aldrich must have prospered despite bad times. In 1802, he dismantled his original log cabin and was able to put up a proper farmhouse. Moses built his home so well that it still stands as part of what is now the Homestead, one of the most celebrated country inns in New England. The roof beams he hewed by hand almost two centuries ago can still be seen in the dining room and first floor parlors.

Seven generations later, the original Moses Aldrich property is still in the same family. Esther Tefft Serafini is now mistress of the Homestead. Essi, as she is known to her friends, is a classic New England innkeeper. New Hampshire born and bred, she is the historian of the area. She can tell you how her ancestors first converted the place into a summer guesthouse in 1880 and how it was finally enlarged to its present size in 1898. Blessed with seemingly total recall, Essi can entertain her guests with stories of famous visitors, such as the time she met Charles Evans Hughes when she was a young girl and sat on the great jurist's lap, playfully pulling at his magisterial white beard.

Essi keeps up with the times. As a licensed real estate broker and a person involved in politics, there is not much that goes on in the

All in the family.

Esther Tefft Serafini, innkeeper of The Homestead, collected clothing from five generations of her family to make her Bicentennial New Hampshire rug, which she designed herself. Antique dolls in freshly laundered dresses, inset, lie in a chest in the hallway of the inn.

THE HOMESTEAD ABOUT 1850. THIS IS THE ORIGINAL FARMHOUSE,
ERECTED IN 1802, BY MOSES ALDRICH, PIONEER SETTLER OF
SUGAR HILL. THIS HAS REMAINED THE FAMILY HOMESTEAD FOR SIX GENERATIONS
1761 — ALDRICH'S FIRST DWELLING WAS A LOG CABIN.

ALDRICH'S DESCENDANTS COMMENCED TO "TAKE SUMMER BOARDERS" IN 1882.

TO ACCOMMODATE AN EXPANDING CLIENTELE, REMODELLING IN 1898

TAKEN ABOUT 1905

DURING REMODELLING — 1898

WAITRESSES OF YESTERYEAR
1905

LOOKING EAST IN THE DINING ROOM, 1927

THE HOMESTEAD, 1947

SAME VIEW AS ABOVE, 1938

Historical hang-ups.

A mounted display of pictures, left, traces the evolution of The Homestead from private farmhouse to inn. Above the piano in the sitting room hangs a picture of the original farm.

Franconia area that she doesn't know about. She is quick to share her local knowledge with her guests and has drawn up detailed instructions for some seventeen motor tours of the area, ranging from a trip to the Great Stone Face at Franconia Notch to a visit to the hunting grounds of Kancamagus, the great seventeenth-century Indian chief. A gracious hostess and a superb cook, she has made up a recipe file of more than fifty New Hampshire specialties for guests who want to try to make them at home. But most of all, Essi is a proper New Englander, direct and observant of certain formalities. She treats her guests as friends, and most of them are, so the atmosphere at the Homestead is one of complete relaxation and informality. The gentlemen coming to dinner in the evening, however, will wear coats and ties.

The Homestead is very much Essi's home. Her family's memorabilia are everywhere. It is possible that during their stay, guests may sleep in the same bed Moses Aldrich had shipped up from Richmond with his wife, Sarah, riding on top of the cart. An informal history of family life at Sugar Hill has been charmingly recaptured on a series of ceramic plates Essi made to illustrate the old-fashioned ways of her forebears, showing scenes ranging from ice skating on the pond to plucking chickens in the old kitchen.

Enzo Serafini, her late husband, is lovingly recalled in family photographs. They ran the Homestead together until his death in 1975. In addition to having a fine touch as an innkeeper, Enzo was a famous ski writer and instructor, who started the first professional ski instruction school in the United States a few miles down the road in Franconia.

By the elegant standards of some of the huge resort facilities that were built in New Hampshire before the turn of the century, the Homestead was just a simple farm guest house. But while the great white elephants perished, the Homestead survived, offering its guests pleasant rooms, good cheer and nourishing food.

The inn itself is spacious, its rooms filled with the results of Essi's skillful foraging at country auctions. Guests have their choice of three types of accommodations. The main house has ten bedrooms on the top two floors with shared baths. Nearby are two more buildings, the Family Cottage and the Chalet. The Chalet, made of heavy timbers, is an architectural delight and a treasure trove of family heirlooms. Its second floor offers two bedrooms and a gigantic living room highlighted by a stone fireplace that burns four-foot logs on cold nights. The Chalet is filled with a priceless collection of wrought iron and eighteenth- and nineteenth-century farm implements. All the accommodations of The Homestead have spectacular views of three distant mountain ranges.

A place for everything.

Innkeeper Esther Serafini's pride and joy is the china and glass collection that fills the shelves of the pine-paneled dining room. It includes glass in the Thousand Eye pattern and some Sandwich glass, above, and Japanese Imari ware on the bottom shelf, opposite.

The texture of time past.

Every element of The Homestead's decoration, no matter what its age, is kept meticulously.

Closing in on seventy, Essi is the very active manager of the Homestead. She does all the furniture repair and restoration work around the place herself, and about half the cooking. Her meals, especially her country breakfasts, are famous all over the country. One family flew all the way from California just for Thanksgiving dinner. When she is not cooking, likely as not Essi will be busy putting up fifty or sixty quarts of preserves at a time. A scrupulous housekeeper, she closes the Homestead for six weeks every spring to give the place a good, old-fashioned New England cleaning. Every item is scrubbed down three times and then polished to a bright finish.

Looking up at the Great Stone Face more than a hundred years ago, Daniel Webster remarked that "The watchmaker hung out a watch to show his trade, but God hung out the Old Man of the Mountains to show that in New Hampshire He made men."

If Esther Tefft Serafini is any indication of His handiwork, God carved out some thoroughly splendid women too.

The view

across the meadow to the mountains is beloved by many generations of guests.

Sitting alone on a rocky point just beyond the village at Perkins Cove, the Island House has been run as an inn since the late 1940s.

ISLAND HOUSE

Perkins Cove, Ogunquit, Maine

We love ice cream, pets, children & barefeet *...and Gordon*

A tourist was drinking in some of the local color around Perkins Cove in Ogunquit one summer afternoon. After watching a few of the weatherbeaten Maine fishermen for a while, the tourist turned to one old-timer and remarked how there surely were a lot of characters around the town.

"Yup," the old-timer replied, "and they all go home on Labor Day."

This anecdote is taken from a delightful local history of Perkins Cove simply titled, with typical Maine efficiency, *The Cove*. It is a perfect Down East story: simple, direct and laced with a piercing Maine wit.

Ogunquit is a classic, tidy little Maine coastal town. Despite the tremendous number of changes that have come in the latter half of the twentieth century, there is a timeless quality about the community. The lobstermen now use synthetic fiber instead of hemp to lash their traps together, but they still fish for lobster pretty much the same way their great-grandfathers did in the early nineteenth century.

Trim as a traditional old Ogunquit dory, the Island House has the feel of a well-run ship. Everything is kept neat and in its place. The living room is decorated with American antiques in a mix of country primitive and functional nautical combined with a few impressive Victorian pieces. Grass and sisal rugs are used throughout, because they are the easiest to keep clean in an ocean-front house. The sand goes right through but stays in one place.

The hall, maintained with a seaman's eye for the utilitarian, has clean, white racks for coats and shelves for other gear. The small office is an efficient working area brightened by shelves containing an impressive collection of Wedgwood china in an Ivanhoe pattern. The floors throughout are not sanded and polished like those in most New

By way of reputation.

With its leisurely lifestyle and striking landscapes, Ogunquit has long attracted seafarers, tourists and some of America's finest artists. Here a visiting yacht ties up in Perkins Cove, where "going ashore" makes for a memorable stopover.

England country inns but are painted like decks on a ship. Upstairs, the rooms could be staterooms in an old schooner. The only riotous note in the whole house is in one of the upstairs rooms which is commanded by a grandiloquent four-poster bed.

The Island House seems ready to put to sea on the morning tide. It is almost entirely surrounded by water and every room in the house has an exceptional view of either Perkins Cove or the Atlantic Ocean; some rooms have a view of both.

Paul and Marge Laurent, the innkeepers, run an extremely personal and pleasant ship. The day begins with a Continental breakfast which Paul prepares in the warm, pine-paneled kitchen and serves in the closed-in porch that doubles as the dining room. After that, the guests are on their own. But that is often enough. Half the fun of staying at the Island House comes when guests meet over breakfast and plan their activities for the day.

There is much to do in Ogunquit during the summer season when

Ship shape.

The Island House is furnished with an eye for the beauty of traditional forms that combine comfort and practicality, as in the inn's sitting room at right. Spanning many periods, the furnishings range from a simple wooden breakfast table, left, to an ornately carved, southern four-poster in one of the bedrooms, above.

the Island House is open. The picturesque seafaring town is ideal for just loafing around and watching the boats nip in and out of the harbor. The swimming on nearby Ogunquit Beach is some of the best in the state but there is also an excellent swimming cove right in back of the inn for those who prefer privacy and don't mind going off the rocks. There are good tennis courts in town and a fine seaside golf course not far away. The Island House does not serve lunch or dinner, but Ogunquit has a number of good restaurants, some just down the road. They feature a variety of seafood dishes including rich chowders, swordfish steak, haddock and, of course, Maine lobster.

The chief attraction in Ogunquit is its busy arts and crafts colony. During its creative heyday, Ogunquit was one of the most important art centers in America. It had its beginning in the late nineteenth century when Charles Woodbury, a famous Massachusetts artist and teacher, journeyed up to the cove in 1889 and found it to be an "artist's paradise." He came there often and founded the Ogunquit Art Association. Hamilton Easter Field, the distinguished artist and critic, came here a few years later and became a driving force in the establishment of Ogunquit as a center of the arts. One of the first important artists he induced to come to Ogunquit was the sculptor Robert Laurent, Paul's father. He made Ogunquit his home and several of his works are still at Island House. Under their leadership, the town became a magnet for most of the important American artists of the day. Painters such as Walt Kuhn, Edward Hopper, George Bellows and Bernard Karfiol came

Sea of tranquility.

In the light of the setting sun, *overleaf,* The Island House is a study in isolation and serenity.

Local color.

Many shops, formerly fishing shacks for Ogunquit seamen, then art studios, are now outlets for the work of local craftsmen. Perkins Cove itself is often the subject of paintings displayed there.

to the cove to share in the artistic excitement and paint its challenging scenery.

At first the local fishermen were a little disconcerted by all this artistic activity, and Mr. Field had to post guards around the life study classes to keep the boys from peeking in, but eventually the two groups got along just fine. The fishermen may not have known much about modern art, but they were good company and prided themselves, with considerable justification, on being the hardest-drinking men in the state. Older citizens of Ogunquit still talk about some of those parties.

Ogunquit may not be the important center of art it once was, and recent construction has altered the face of the community, but the change has been gradual. Every summer Ogunquit bursts with color from the local art shows and gallery exhibitions.

The future is uncertain, as it always is for seafarers. But for now, the Island House continues to be that greatest of all seamen's blessings, a safe harbor.

ASTICOU INN

Northeast Harbor, Maine

The Asticou Inn has been the most prominent landmark in Northeast Harbor for almost eighty years. Set well up on a hill above the town, this large, comfortable inn is a venerable institution in a community that knows how to honor its treasures. In fact, the Asticou Inn is owned by a group of local citizens who bought the place in order to ensure it would be maintained in the traditional manner. Thanks to them, and to manager George M. Stiles, the inn has been modernized and expanded, and the tradition of gracious innkeeping goes on as before. Guests and townspeople can still enjoy the sweeping views of the harbor and the ocean beyond from Asticou's spacious porch, and the tradition of "dinner at the Asticou" for the sumptuous Thursday night buffet remains a ritual social event in the town.

There is nothing very fancy about the Asticou. It is not gussied up with special effects. It is the kind of honest, down-to-earth place one would expect to find in Maine. The lobby is large but seems more like a living room, with its wing chairs flanking a handsome white fireplace. Upstairs, the rooms are simply and conservatively furnished. Many of them have bay windows facing out onto the sparkling harbor below. For guests desiring more privacy, there are excellent individual cottages on the property. Although Asticou is open only from mid-June through mid-September, its sister facility, the Cranberry Lodge, provides accommodations for the rest of the year.

The Asticou's chief attraction comes not from what it is but from where it is—on Mt. Desert Island, where some of the most beautiful country anywhere is surrounded by some of the bluest water in the world. Ever since Samuel de Champlain first mapped it in 1604, this little island has attracted all kinds of people to its hospitable shores.

A good place to be.

A terrace along the east front of the Asticou's shingled bulk provides a view of the harbor, which is seen also from the inn's lounge, above. At the base of the sprawling lawns are formal flower beds.

A northern landscape.

In the forest on Eliot Mountain, an evergreen skeleton filters the setting sun. The swimming pool accommodates guests for whom the cold Atlantic water is too much to contemplate. Tamed into ordered beauty, the grounds of Thuya Garden, a short hike from the inn, add Oriental calm to Mount Desert's stark beauty.

Colonial conventions.

The muraled wall, severe chairs, and chandelier of the Asticou's dining room recall old New England traditions. The menu hews to satisfying fare carefully served. Pan-fried fish is often available at breakfast, and fish lightly sauced is a dinner feature.

Artists come to paint, and writers come to write. Yachtsmen come to sail, and others just come to relax in a rocker on the veranda of the Asticou. Sooner or later, however, the brisk Maine air energizes even the most sedentary guests, and there is much to see and do on the island. On the opposite side is well-known Bar Harbor. The town was originally called Eden, and some people love the spot so much they think it was wrong to change the name.

Golfers must take a whack at the course at the Kebo Valley Club, the oldest links in the state. This tough little layout was a favorite of champion golf pro Walter Hagen, who held the local course record for many years. Those who play badly at Kebo can console themselves with the knowledge that the seventh hole is named after President William Howard Taft, who once negotiated it in twenty-seven shots.

The drive to the top of Cadillac Mountain provides motorists with some of the most awesome views on the East Coast. Cadillac and the Ocean Drive along the shore are only two of the spectacular features of Acadia National Park. Because it is situated near the top of the temperate zone, Acadia exhibits an extraordinary variety of plant and animal life, along with other natural phenomena. As John Cole of the *Maine Times* once wrote, Acadia is "an incredible combining of the fragile and the violent, the contorted and the calm, the shattered and the serene. Here nature can be found at her most sublime—and most contentious."

Pilgrim's Inn's ample bulk may have prompted the name "The Ark," which it was called when run as a summer boarding house.

PILGRIM'S INN

Deer Isle, Maine

Many New England country inns seem to be forever frozen in time, images of a particular period in history. A few manage to convey a sense of their long heritage and still be very much twentieth-century establishments. The Pilgrim's Inn on Deer Isle, Maine, is one of those few.

The original structure was erected in 1793, under somewhat unusual circumstances, and has been going its own quixotic way ever since. The first owner of the property was Ignatius Haskell. Squire Haskell was a prominent Maine businessman who helped frame the state's Constitution. He had a successful sawmill on Deer Isle and decided to build his home near his business. Mrs. Haskell, however, was accustomed to the refinements of life in Newburyport and balked at the idea. She told her husband that she would not live in a Maine wilderness without properly civilized accommodations. So the easy-going squire had a proper mansion constructed in Newburyport and then shipped up to Deer Isle where it was immediately acknowledged to be the finest home anyone on the island had ever seen.

Over the years, the building has changed with the times. Originally a classic double-chimneyed Georgian house, it picked up a then-stylish Greek Revival addition in the 1820s. It gained a front porch somewhere along the line when such things were fashionable; however, when the fashion changed, the porch was lost.

The Pilgrim's Inn today carries on in that eclectic tradition. The marvelous downstairs common room with its walk-in fireplace is furnished with a combination of period pieces and comfortable modern sofas that seem to get along together quite well. The inn is still heated entirely by stoves and wood-burning fireplaces just as it was almost

Peaceful harbor.

A stone-raised causeway runs between Deer Isle's harbor and Ignatius Haskell's tidal mill pond. Here it is shown on a wonderfully damp, foggy fall day.

A delicate balance.

There's something for everyone in this mélange of styles, ranging from the late Victorian desk and chair above to the sprawling Victorian couch set below a somber modern painting. More modern furniture stands before the original fireplace in the common room, while the bedrooms all blend modern paintings with a variety of furnishings.

two centuries ago, but the accommodations are modern and convenient enough to have pleased even old Mrs. Haskell. Much of the original paneling and woodwork is still in place, but the paintings on the walls are fine examples of contemporary art, many chosen from the work of the artists who live in the area.

The upstairs rooms are a convivial mixture of styles, and overnight guests may find themselves sleeping on an Early American four-poster or a French Empire sleigh bed. In one area, Pilgrim's Inn is charmingly out of sorts with most traditional innkeeping: the bathrooms are huge, and one tub is long enough for the tallest of men to stretch out in.

The innkeepers, George and Eleanor Pavloff, instill an air of happy informality at Pilgrim's Inn. A pair of springer spaniels have the run of the house. Sooner or later overnight guests are almost sure to find themselves in the kitchen, and dinner at the Pilgrim's Inn is like a family house party. Eleanor serves hot hors d'oeuvres and paté in the common room, and the guests all get to know one another before going into the old barn for dinner, where, likely as not, they will find their table in what once was a goat stall.

Deer Isle is just off the coast of Maine, and although the mainland is easily accessible by car, most guests prefer to stay put during their stay. The island has a large number of expert silversmiths, weavers and potters, whose studios are open for browsing. The antiques shops are friendly, and the Deer Isle–Stonington Historical Society on the western side of the island maintains a delightful series of exhibits on the early life of coastal Maine. Adventurous guests can go clamming or play golf or tennis at the Island Country Club. But for many, the most enjoyable activity, as George and Eleanor say, is to "do nothing, pleasantly."

A scale of values.

Informality is the style at Pilgrim's Inn, where guests sometimes make themselves at home in the kitchen. These fresh vegetables and herbs were grown just outside in the kitchen garden; the meals at the inn are truly "garden fresh."

What can we use it for?

Deer Isle's thrift turns a broken lobster pot into a planter, waste wood into a hobby horse, and an old barn into the romantic dining room at right. During colder months, dinner is served in the inn's more formal dining room indoors.

Maine gold.

A big-bayed dowager of a building, the inn sits among maples at the top of a small hill. The Craftsman clock and Victorian Gothic chair, inset, stand in the inn's upstairs hallway.

Social butterfly.

The French cuisine of Le Papillon, the inn's restaurant, was unusual for the area when it opened. The idea of skiers fresh off the slopes consuming coquille St. Jacques Parisienne, tournedos Henri IV, and châteaubriand Béarnaise was new, but Le Papillon is now one of several fine restaurants in the Maine ski areas.

Grand design.

Maple balusters carry the curving staircase rail, *overleaf*. From a landing lit by a Palladian window, the stairs sweep to the lobby in a wide, straight run. The Chickering box grand piano and the sofas in the hall are older than the house.

WINTER'S INN
Kingfield, Maine

Francis and Freelan Stanley were as remarkable a pair of brothers as New England ever saw. Identical twins with matching beards, they always dressed exactly alike, from their flowered ties and stickpins to their British bowlers. The brothers were marvelously inventive, if somewhat impractical. They dabbled in making violins and also developed a photographic plate process that they later sold to George Eastman, helping him start the Kodak camera empire. The brothers' most famous contribution to society was the Stanley Steamer automobile, the fastest American car on wheels during its heyday in the early 1900s.

The twins were also given to sudden impulses. One afternoon in the 1890s, while they and their friend Amos Winter were trying to think of something to do, Freelan suggested, "Let's build a house up there on that hill." They immediately set to work designing a stately Georgian Colonial Revival mansion, which Amos liked so much he eventually moved in.

For such an inventive pair, their first attempt at architecture was quite typical of the times. Their only two eccentricities were a huge heating system, designed around a giant furnace that had once been a railroad engine boiler, and plans for a steam-driven elevator that fortunately was never incorporated into the construction of the house.

Under the direction of its present-day owner, Michael Thom, a local architect by way of Toronto, the Winter's Inn encourages an easygoing, twentieth-century lifestyle amid elegant, nineteenth-century surroundings. The largest part of its clientele are skiers, who like to relax when they come off the slopes of nearby Sugarloaf and Saddleback mountains. Entering the side of the building, skiers find a long corridor called the "bowling alley," which is used for hanging up wet gear;

Premium space.

Bold wallpaper and a big brass bed impose only a little on the large room at left above, whose windows look over the town. Above, Mount Abram, its long ridge touched with clouds, rises serenely at the limit of the wide valley. The goat by the pool was a playful gift to innkeeper Michael Thom.

Hearthside.

Warm center of the house, the hall fireplace is flanked by portraits ascribed to Nathaniel Hone on the left and Joseph Wright of Derby on the right.

upstairs, on the top floor, is a skiers' dormitory. But in between is a series of rooms that recalls the times when Amos Winter lived in the finest home in Kingfield.

The earth-toned downstairs rooms are amply proportioned and show off their Neo-Georgian heritage with a series of delicately made pillars, and a trio of matching fireplaces. Coming in the oak front door, with an elaborate W etched into the glass, guests find themselves in a high, wide hall. On the right is the bar, a smallish room with a large bay window looking out on tall maples that screen the inn from the town below. On the left of the hallway are the two rooms that make up the inn's stylish French restaurant, Le Papillon.

This part of the country is famous for its skiing, but there is much to do the rest of the year, as well. The nearby mountains offer some challenging hiking, and many of the young employees at Winter's Inn can give firsthand information about the trails in the area. For the less athletic, there are county fairs at Farmington and North New Portland in the late summer and early fall. One matchless natural event occurs every spring—the main stream and the west branch of the Carrabassett River join just below the inn, and after the winter there is usually an ice jam at their confluence. As spring approaches, the ice starts to crack and groan so loudly that even the guests inside the inn can hear it. The townspeople line the banks waiting for the ice to break. Suddenly, with a tremendous roar, the ice field splits open and rushes downstream. That incomparable season known as the Maine Summer is beginning.

Mixed metaphors.

The Rossmount, four flags flying at its front, reminds some people of a sleek British sailing vessel. Others see it as a crouching British lion.

ROSSMOUNT INN
St. Andrews-by-the-Sea, New Brunswick

New Brunswick is Loyalist country. After the American Revolution, many colonials who still swore allegiance to King George came here to begin life in the New World once again. The Rossmount Inn, which has been a traveler's hotel in the Passamaquoddy Bay area for almost one hundred years, proclaims that heritage proudly. The inn crouches on the hill below Chamcook Mountain like the British lion. Its rooms are filled with a wealth of period pieces from all over the world. There is a plaster reproduction of the Winged Victory of Samothrace, a piano originally made for Kaiser Wilhelm that got rerouted during World War I and found its way to Rossmount, and several examples of French Provincial furniture. But the tone throughout the inn is unmistakably British. A small bronze statue of William Shakespeare stands at the foot of the massive main stairway. Staffordshire dogs seem to be in every room. A proper English pub dart board is always at the ready in the taproom. A chair used by the King of Belgium at the coronation of Queen Elizabeth II is in the front hall. The famous Karsh portrait of the Queen hangs in the front parlor. The focal point of the dining room is an alcove of three stained-glass windows taken from an eighteenth-century English chapel. The windows, casting an orange glow over the room, depict the symbols of the three early kingdoms of Great Britain: the English rose, the Irish harp and the Scottish thistle.

The sun will never set on the British Empire so long as the Rossmount Inn has anything to say about it.

It is axiomatic among innkeepers that the key to success is personal management, and few managers carry that tradition further than George and Marion Brewin. With their two preteen children, the Brewins literally do everything. George runs the inn, tends the bar and

Royal regalia.

A piano originally intended for Kaiser Wilhelm II sits in the Rossmount's bar, beneath chromos of English royalty and the portrait of John Syme, Sr., the former innkeeper's father.

personally cooks the breakfast. Marion cooks all of the dinners herself, including making her own breads and pastries, soups and desserts. When it is dinnertime, the children put on their best clothes and help serve.

Whether his guests are world-famous statesmen—Prime Minister Lester Pearson and President Lyndon Johnson have stayed overnight—a sales convention, honeymooners or just old friends coming back year after year, George provides the animating spirit of the Rossmount Inn. His personal stamp is all-pervasive. Although the inn backs up on eighty-seven acres of forest, George has forbidden any hunting in the area. As a result guests can now see deer, black bear and moose feeding in the wild. There is no gift shop at the Rossmount, and George will not even sell a picture postcard, because he feels such frivolities tend to cheapen a fine old inn. An active believer in physical fitness, George jogs every morning with his family, and he encourages his guests to take as much exercise as possible. There is a jogging trail on the property and plenty of other opportunities for exercise, from swimming

Loyal
to the realm.

The Rossmount reception hall welcomes guests into a museum of Anglophile devotion. The mirror in the bar, above, recalls an Edwardian pub. Solid comfort in a Rossmount bedroom, right, encourages long stays, no matter what the weather.

in the Rossmount's heated pool to golfing on the championship course at nearby St. Andrews-by-the-Sea. For willing souls, George suggests a hike up Chamcook Mountain. The view of the islands, estuaries and small lakes dotted among the foothills is well worth the effort. For the less energetic, St. Andrews offers some charming streets for an afternoon stroll while shopping for English woolens and Scottish tweeds.

George is very picky about the food served at the Rossmount. For fish, the inn features haddock, Atlantic salmon and pollack freshly caught in the Passamaquoddy Bay. No bottom fish, such as flounder, are served, because George feels they have to be cooked too long and lose their marvelous fresh flavor. George has also forbidden grain-fed beef to be served at the Rossmount. Instead he offers only the leaner, grass-fed variety. Most of the vegetables come from the Brewins' own gardens. In the summer, the whole family goes out to the hills in the back to gather fresh strawberries for the table.

English to the core, George has a cockney accent that still rings with the sound of Bowbells. Nonetheless, he has become an admirer of the American transcendentalists. Mottoes of Ralph Waldo Emerson and Henry Thoreau are on the walls of many of the rooms in the Rossmount, and George talks familiarly of the epigrams of "Old Ralph Waldo." George has had to work hard to preserve the unique spirit of the Rossmount Inn. He closes for more winter months than he'd like— because of soaring fuel costs—but his self-reliant vigor has kept the Victorian hostelry shined and welcoming, a place where personal service is still taken seriously.

76

A cornucopia of hospitality.

The dining room's stained-glass alcove provides a regal setting for some of the Rossmount's crystal and silver. The whole room, a part of which is shown below, has an atmosphere of Victorian domesticity raised to a splendorous level.

At the piano in the sitting room the innkeepers' son, Gregor Read, brings new spirit to an old classical ballad.

MARSHLANDS INN

Sackville, New Brunswick

Serenade of silver.

The Read family collection of silver is famed throughout Canada, and sterling silver place settings are *de rigeur*.

Hundreds of years ago the Indians, watching in wonder as millions of migrating waterfowl flew in and out of the marshland area of what is now New Brunswick, called the swelling noise they made *tintamarro* ("sound of bird wings"). That roaring sound can still be heard today from the huge flocks of geese and ducks that make this unique part of Canada their home.

The Tantramar marshes have remained completely unspoiled over the centuries, and the perfect spot to enjoy their wild beauty is the Marshlands Inn, an oasis of civilized gentility in the rugged Canadian countryside. Built in the 1850s, the house was bought in 1895 by Henry C. Read as his family home. In those days, Mr. Read ran a prosperous stone-cutting business, and it was his boast that every tool in Canada had been sharpened on a Read stone. In the 1920s, the business declined when synthetically bonded abrasives such as Carborundum replaced natural grindstones. But the enterprising Read family realized they had a tremendous asset in their home; it was converted into a country inn in 1935 and has remained in the family ever since.

There are many lures for travelers in this part of the country: birdwatching, excellent golfing, hiking and swimming, along with a spectacular view in Moncton of the famous tidal bore, caused by the extreme tides in the nearby Bay of Fundy. But not the least of the attractions is the Marshlands Inn itself. A big, rambling country house with a majestic silver birch tree out front, the inn is an ideal spot for getting away from the modern world without giving up any of its comforts. The sun porch, shaded by a row of ferns, is a pleasant place for just daydreaming in the afternoon; the twin parlors, each with its own fireplace and furnished with a variety of cozy wing chairs and

Hot chocolate and homemade gingersnaps are an evening ritual designed to satisfy those nocturnal cravings while warming guests up for a peaceful slumber.

Victorian sofas, invite conversation between fellow guests in the evening. The spacious dining room is illuminated by nineteenth-century pewter chandeliers, and the service is from impeccable Spode and the Reads' own family silverware. Some of the bedrooms upstairs are quite small, but a few are really magnificent affairs. One of the most impressive is a bed/sitting room dominated by a comfortable old four-poster. For cold nights, the Marshlands keeps a supply of lush, satin quilts.

In addition to its gracious appointments, the Marshlands Inn offers some of the finest cooking anywhere in the Maritime Provinces. Everything is homemade. The breakfasts are typically hearty Canadian country fare, offering baked apples, cracked-wheat porridge, creamed salt cod, kippered herring, Maple Leaf bacon, stacks of buckwheat pancakes, fresh breads and a homemade gooseberry jelly that looks like jade. For dinner, the Marshlands Inn offers traditional regional meals, such as steak and kidney pie, haddock chowder and Atlantic salmon from Newfoundland. Its most sought-after dish is an order of fiddleheads dripping with butter. An early growth of the ostrich fern, fiddleheads are grown wild in New Brunswick and are shipped to gourmet shops all over the world. Fiddleheads are virtually the national vegetable of Canada and are served at all state banquets held by the governor-general. They taste best, however, at the Marshlands Inn, where they are served freshly picked.

The slogan of the Marshlands Inn is "more like a club," and Herbert Read prides himself on offering personal touches that are rarely found in commercial hotels. The bureau in each bedroom shows the extent of his concern for his guests: each contains a gentleman's two-foot-long shoehorn; an old-fashioned pin cushion complete with pins, needles and thread for quick repairs; and even an extra pair of shoelaces. Every evening at ten o'clock, he serves hot cocoa and cookies in the front parlor for guests who need something to tide them over until breakfast.

No wonder that, like the magnificent Canadian geese overhead, people keep coming back to the Marshlands Inn every spring.

On top of the world

is a huge attic bedroom with two double beds and a single bed, two windowseats and a Victorian sofa and chairs. The other bedrooms display the magnificent antiques and delightful wallpapers found throughout the inn.

KILMUIR PLACE

Northeast Margaree, Cape Breton, Nova Scotia

"It's just home," says Isabel Taylor, the beautiful, white-haired innkeeper, as she gestures toward the table in the kitchen while her guests wander in and out, inquiring about dinner, snitching a piece of chocolate cake or just sitting down to talk about what lures will be best for the next day's salmon fishing.

Kilmuir Place, named for a parish house on the Isle of Skye off the northwest coast of Scotland, has been Isabel's home all of her life. Her husband, Ross, is a relative newcomer; he has only lived there for the last fifty years. Together they run the most informal country inn imaginable. There are only five guest rooms in Kilmuir; so people must make reservations long in advance. When visitors arrive, they will find a rustic country inn, utterly without pretension. It is a square white farmhouse with a bit of ivy clinging to it. There's a gray, weathered barn a few yards away. The laundry flaps gaily on the line out back. The guests sometimes lend a hand around the house. If after dinner some want to take their own plates back to the kitchen, Isabel will not stand in their way. But the guests will also get service that the Ritz-Carlton cannot match. Bring back a fresh-caught salmon or trout from the nearby waters, and Isabel will cook it to order. Ross bakes the cakes, and waiting upstairs in the bedrooms is that all-but-forgotten amenity, hand-ironed sheets.

The small farmhouse is furnished almost entirely with family pieces, and Isabel can recount the history of each one: the spool bed, she had brought in by wheelbarrow; the dining room table was her grandmother's; the sheepskin rug came from the local flock. The hooked rug with a seagull motif and the hooked rug runners upstairs were made by a neighbor's fifteen-year-old son. Isabel's favorite color is red, so the kitchen has a red table and red-and-white checked curtains made

Isabel's red wheelbarrow.

Every item at Kilmuir has a story, even a red wheelbarrow hidden away by the barn. Isabel Taylor used it to bring a spool bed from her Grandmother Taylor's house nearby. Red, Isabel's favorite color, brightens the front door, the kitchen table, and several other spots in addition to this lowly wheelbarrow.

God's little acre.

In the heart of what many call "God's Country," the inn can just be recognized by its red door in the center of the Cape Breton landscape above.

Join the family.

Innkeeper Isabel Taylor, who was born here, takes guests under her wing and shares the family treasures: Mother's wedding dishes, top left; Grandma's lovely red manicure set, bottom right; her sewing room, always sunny, bottom left.

by an American guest while her husband was off fishing. The large oval bowl under the low table in the living room comes from the governor's mansion in Maine.

"Everything we have here is family," Isabel explains. The house is filled with charming down-home touches: little piggy banks, flowered needlepoint, white organdy curtains and a collection of cowbells. As if she were putting out goodies for visiting grandchildren, Isabel sees to it that a tray in the living room is always filled with chocolates, peanuts and mints to nibble on. And for those who can't wait until the proper mealtime, Isabel will fix a sandwich.

Mealtimes at Kilmuir are as pleasantly informal as the house itself. Guests can sit at the dining table if they wish, but at breakfast many enjoy having Isabel's strong coffee and fresh blueberry muffins in the kitchen, where there is plenty of room to tie flies and get advice from Ross on where the salmon are biting.

At dinner, all the guests join Ross and Isabel in the dining room. The food is all farm fresh, since Isabel and Ross grow most of their own vegetables: peas, green and yellow beans, squash, corn and potatoes. "We do the picking," Ross quips, "and you do the eating."

Besides cooking freshly caught fish, Isabel provides old-fashioned Nova Scotia fare for dinner: roast beef, crabmeat casserole, salmon mousse, cranberry pudding, rolled-oat bread on the side and possibly a fresh mince pie or one made with raspberries and cherries.

The Nova Scotia countryside is among the most blessed spots on earth. This is the land of the Acadians that Henry Wadsworth Longfellow immortalized in *Evangeline*. The Cabot Trail, named after the great English explorer who may have first seen this island as early as 1497, runs through Cape Breton, providing motorists with spectacular views of both the Gulf of St. Lawrence and the Atlantic Ocean.

The flavor of the area now is largely Scottish, and during the summer season there is enough activity going on to gladden the heart of the stoutest highlander. The traditional Gathering of the Clans and the Fisherman's Regatta take place on Dominion Day, July 1. Later that

85

month, Scottish athletes descend on Antigonish for the annual Highland Games. The most spectacular event of the games is "Tossing the Caber," a lunatic enterprise in which a man throws a telephone pole as far as he can. It is something only a Scot could be talked into doing. The Festival of the Tartans is held in New Glasgow in August.

Closer to Kilmuir Place, the pleasures are more simple. In addition to matchless hiking trails, there are several interesting museums nearby that have good collections of local artifacts.

Directly in front of Kilmuir, there is an old-fashioned wishing well—but there isn't much more to wish for. The air is crisp and clean, and the salmon are running off Cape Breton. The countryside is blooming with wild flowers, and there is a little white church down the road. Ross is chopping some firewood, and Isabel is in the kitchen making an apple pie for dinner tonight.

As Isabel says, "No matter how far you have traveled, when you're at Kilmuir, you're home."

86

Unmistakably "country."

From the tweeds, umbrellas and walking sticks to the washing flapping on the line under a glowering sky, there is no doubt about it: this is the country and these are the Scots. Napoleon looks down on it all disapprovingly, of course.

WHEATLEIGH

Lenox, Massachusetts

When most Americans think of "a little place in the country," they generally conjure up a vision of a small cottage tucked away from the busy city, with perhaps a white picket fence, and a bed of petunias near the door. Well, the wealthy and titled need a little peace and quiet, too. So when the daughter of American industrialist H. H. Cook married the Count de Heredia of Italy in the 1920s, her father gave her a little place in the country for a wedding present—his thirty-two room Italianate palazzo on 250 acres of rolling Berkshire hillside.

Crowning a rise south of Lenox, this magnificent residence, with its sprawling grounds, manicured gardens and panoramic views of the surrounding countryside, was the showplace of the Berkshires. By the time David Weisgal and Florence Brooks-Dunay discovered it in 1976, the elegant pile had grown somewhat shabby since it was sold by the Countess's heirs in 1949. Land speculators had bought up all but twenty-one acres of the original property, and the main building showed the wear and tear of almost thirty years of service, first as a summer dormitory facility for the Boston Symphony Orchestra, then as a local arts center.

"When we first saw it," Florence recalls, "the house was like a battered child; used and abused in every detail."

Still, the couple had a connoisseur's eye for fine line and could see the mansion's beauty behind the disarray. Fortunately for the old house, they had the vision and the resources to retrieve it. David put down $235,000 to buy the estate and very quickly spent another $100,000 on painting, cleaning and initial restoration.

Later that same year, they reopened the mansion as Wheatleigh, perhaps the most imposing country inn in America. Neither David nor Florence had any experience as innkeepers—David had been a successful executive involved in fund raising and philanthropic estate management and Florence had been a professional dancer. But good innkeeping is often as much a matter of the spirit as anything else, and David and Florence have that indispensable quality in abundance. "We didn't really look on this as a commercial enterprise," David said. "We bought it mainly for a change, a new way of life. It is an extension of ourselves. I think of it as our home, to which people are invited as guests."

Florence took responsibility for the redecoration of Wheatleigh and brought a light, modern touch to bear on the baronial mansion. The noble aspect of the rooms and the splendor of their details—such as the ornately carved chimneybreasts and twenty-five-foot high ceilings—have been retained but brought charmingly down to more manageable proportions with the use of lots of wicker and crisp, modern fabrics. There is still a large percentage of ornate Renaissance furniture, but it

Going up in the world.

Lit by stained-glass windows, Wheatleigh's main staircase rises grandly towards the inn's sleeping quarters.

State of the art.

The Palladian grandeur of Wheatleigh's limestone, terra-cotta and marble arcade, above, is complemented by the simplicity of an outdoor pine dining table. The wooden ceiling of the loggia, left, is a small part of the craftsmanship of 150 Italian workmen imported to fashion ceilings, mantels and walls. *Overleaf*, a winged sculpture sits on a lawn below the south terrace.

is now mixed with lighter pieces of David and Florence's own. David does much of the heavy work. He personally greets the guests, carries their luggage upstairs and fetches the firewood. In the morning, he is often on hand to make the omelets himself, and in the evening, he may be behind the bar making cocktails.

The rooms at Wheatleigh come in two varieties: regular and deluxe. The regular rooms are often quite small and simple, but the deluxe accommodations are simply spectacular. As an overnight guest at Wheatleigh, visitors might find themselves awakening in a vast, sunstruck white room with canopied beds, thick rugs, wicker chairs and a gigantic fireplace graced with a frieze of sculpted birds. French doors lead onto a private terrace, looking toward the gardens and the swimming pool. A duplex suite called the Aviary has a central spiral staircase connecting the two floors. There is a wood-burning stove to warm the suite during the cool Berkshire evenings, and plenty of comfortable sofas and lounge chairs, although when Leonard Bernstein stays in the Aviary, he has the sofas taken out and a grand piano brought in.

The ornamentation throughout the house and grounds is breathtaking. According to family legend, when Mr. Cook set about in 1893 to recreate a sixteenth-century Florentine palace in the Berkshires, he did not stint. Mr. Cook reputedly spent $1 million for construction alone, and an additional, unrecorded sum for landscaping. In order to ensure accuracy of design and detail, he imported 150 Italian craftsmen to carve the ceilings, mantels and walls. As a million dollars' worth of work tends to do, it shows. The house is filled with elegant, Old World, nineteenth-century flourishes. But thanks to David and Florence's good taste and sense of style, they do not seem old-fashioned, but timelessly elegant, and ideally suited for modern lifestyles.

Wheatleigh has both indoor and outdoor dining rooms. In the summer, the outdoor room, a screened-in pergola just off the terrace, is a delightful place for lunch. Breakfast and dinner are served in a

91

Wheatleigh's grounds

are magnificent. Situated atop a rise, the mansion commands a majestic view of the Berkshires.

Uncompromising splendor.

The wrought-iron and glass canopy over the front entrance shows the care paid to architectural detail.

beautifully simple indoor dining room, where Florence has hung plants at all of the arched windows, spread a carpet with a cabbage rose design and brought in round tables and bentwood chairs. Breakfast at Wheatleigh is a civilized affair, where guests are served as late as 10:00 A.M., a relief from so many places where guests are expected to be up and about the affairs of the day by nine at the latest. In the evening, dinner is served on tables set with tulip glasses, rich red napery, fresh flowers and candles. The cuisine is a combination of Continental and American fare. The entrees are usually standards of the French and Italian repertoire, but the dessert most experienced guests select is the chef's own homemade pecan pie.

**Inner
peace.**
The French desk and
Windsor chair provide a
serene writing spot.

**The
view**
from Wheatleigh's largest
bedroom includes
Stockbridge Bowl.

Wheatleigh's bar, in the old library, boasts a sculptured chimneypiece. In the summer, the bar is cool and quiet, and in the winter, its blazing fire, glinting off the polished wood and glass of the bookcases, makes for a warmly pleasant end to a day of cross-country skiing.

There is a swimming pool and a tennis court on the property, and facilities for golfing, horseback riding, fishing, ice skating and skiing are all nearby. Additionally, Wheatleigh is uniquely situated to take advantage of the many cultural events for which the area is world famous. The Boston Symphony makes its summer home at Tanglewood, a ten-minute walk away, and the jazz and folk concerts at Music Inn are just down the hill. The Berkshire Playhouse, Jacob's Pillow Dance Festival and the enchanting chamber music programs offered by the South Mountain concert series are all within a half-hour's drive.

But the main attraction for most of the guests at Wheatleigh is Wheatleigh itself. After all, as David says, "It is a fantasy come true."

Pillow Dance festivals are likely to be seen in one of the convivial taprooms. When people at the inn occasionally look familiar, the chances are they've been seen in Norman Rockwell paintings. Rockwell lives in Stockbridge and seems to have used almost everyone in the town as a model at one time or another.

The Red Lion Inn has had a long, and sometimes troubled, history. After a succession of owners, it was bought, in 1862, by Mr. and Mrs. Charles Plumb, whose family operated the establishment for more than ninety years. Mrs. Plumb lavished care and great affection on the establishment, filling it with a priceless collection of antiques, china and pewter, much of which is still on display. The inn burned to the ground in 1896 but was rebuilt by the Plumb family on the original site. In 1968, the historic old place was almost torn down to make room for a supermarket but was saved at the last minute by John and Jane Fitzpatrick, who still operate it.

Going through the inn today, guests can only be eternally grateful that this charming old building was saved. The lobby is large and wide but so well organized and neatly furnished that it has the coziness of a small New England sitting room. Amidst all the comings and goings of the guests, there is still time to relax on one of the many Victorian sofas. The room features a huge fireplace, decorated with a striking collection of antique keys. Several antique cupboards contain some of Mrs. Plumb's finest china. There is also an extensive collection of teapots in all styles and varieties.

Festival of lights.

In the evening the dining room glows with chandeliers, each with a cascade of faceted crystal pendants. Below, a German painting of a forest scene hangs above the sideboard at one end of the room. Fresh flowers are provided for the tables year-round.

101

Down to the last detail.

These antique teapots at the foot of the main stairway are part of Mrs. Plumb's vast collection.

Spacious and splendid.

The Red Lion Inn has over one hundred rooms. The corner suite below contains antique Victorian furnishings of which the inn is particularly proud.

Guests going upstairs have their choice of walking up a delicately balustered Colonial Revival staircase or being transported by way of a silver-painted cage elevator that looks like a nineteenth-century antique, and, indeed, is only a few years shy of being exactly that. But it has been successfully carrying guests and their luggage upstairs for as long as anyone can remember.

The main rooms, along with the more than one hundred bedrooms and the halls upstairs, are dotted with dozens of delightful surprises. Along one of the downstairs halls is a large Victorian breakfront displaying a large set of crystal with red lions cut into the handles of the compotes and bowls. It was made especially for the inn during the nineteenth century. In the dining room, the inn uses a modern version of Blue Willow for its china, and pewter serving plates displaying the Red Lion crest. The walls throughout the inn are filled with fine examples of American popular art since the late nineteenth century. The inn has not tried to make a museum out of its art collection, but those guests who wish to do so can trace the development of commercial art from the enchanting Victorian illustrations in *Godey's Lady's Book,* to genre engraving by Currier and Ives and their contemporaries, on to the present-day master of illustration, Norman Rockwell. Not surprisingly, the inn features many works by the most famous of Stockbridge's resident artists. Among the most fetching are some of the early drawings Rockwell did for a special edition of *Tom Sawyer.* Wherever one turns in the Red Lion Inn, whether it is to look at the stained-glass windows illuminating the dark wood-paneled pub room

103

Let there be fall.
White wicker in the inn's courtyard recalls summer amid the splendors of a Berkshire autumn.

in the Widow Bingham Tavern, or one of the authentic Franklin stoves in the bedrooms, there is some charming grace note to be seen.

Originally a simple wayside stopover, the Red Lion Inn, as with so many other historic places, now finds itself in the middle of a busy community. Although it still retains all of its old, country charm, the inn is now also a center in a year-round resort area. In the spring, the Berkshire hills come alive as only the New England countryside can. The summer is a busy sporting time, with several golf and tennis facilities nearby. This is also the time for the world-famous festivals at the Berkshire Playhouse, Jacob's Pillow and Tanglewood. In the fall, the New England foliage is so glorious that tourists who cannot find lodging at the Red Lion, or at one of the many other facilities in the area, are more than willing to be put up at the local jail for the night— if there's room in the jail.

In the winter, the Berkshires are a major ski area. At Christmastime the Red Lion becomes, perhaps, its most appealing. The inn blossoms out with garlands of greenery, and holiday wreaths appear in the hallways and public rooms. The Fitzpatricks' daughter, Ann, an experienced confectioner who operates her own candy store, creates a replica of the Red Lion Inn made entirely of Christmas goodies, and carolers put in several appearances during the season to sing around the huge Christmas tree set up in the front parlor.

With all of its delights and attention to the well-being of its guests,

the Red Lion is accustomed to getting good reviews. One of the earliest known was written sometime in the 1850s and is on record at the Laurel Hill Association, a local historical society: "The Stockbridge House, now open for transients, guests and summer boarders," wrote the correspondent, "has been put in perfect order from garret to cellar, and with its open fireplaces, its quaint, comfortable furniture, and ancient bric-a-brac, and with Plumb as landlord, it offers a delightful abode, seldom to be found in a country village."

Some 125 years later, in 1977, the Red Lion Inn got another review, which it probably prizes the most of all. It was from John Ticknor, who has visited the inn regularly during his long life. He remembers first sitting on the veranda of the Red Lion in 1887 when he was three years old. The main street of Stockbridge was then a dirt road that the local farmers used as a cow trail. Mr. Ticknor returned to the inn every single summer for the next ninety years. He recalls the days at the turn of the century when, every afternoon at four, "the wealthy people used to go up and down Main Street. Then they would all go somewhere for a cocktail." A great many of them would then come to the Red Lion Inn for dinner, and in those days, Mr. Ticknor remembers, "anybody who would think of going to dinner without a tuxedo would be shot at sunrise. The inn had a solid clientele. It was a social center."

The Red Lion Inn is still a social center, and now, after more than two hundred years of almost continual service, it is, according to Mr. Ticknor, "better than ever."

On the face of it.

The building's peculiar facade is intriguing, recalling sometimes colonial townhouses, sometimes the spaciousness of Victorian buildings. The porches of the inn are decorated appropriate to each holiday season.

PUBLICK HOUSE
Sturbridge, Massachusetts

Ebenezer Crafts was one of those extraordinary men the American Revolution needed so desperately. A fierce fighter and a mountain of a man—it was said he drank cider by lifting the barrel and taking it straight from the bunghole—Crafts was also pious, scholarly and, in business matters, astute. All of these qualities were required to see him and the colonies through the darkest days of the Revolution.

Born in Pomfret, Connecticut, in 1740, Crafts studied theology at Yale, and hoped to become a minister. When no parish call came, he moved to Sturbridge in 1770, and built a store and tavern. In those days the local publican was one of the principal figures in the community. According to one informal history of the area, "He was the businessman, frequently the banker, who travelled to Boston or to Providence, even to New York. When he returned, his wagon was laden with supplies from the city, and he was overflowing with news. Both good news and bad news he retailed to the eager villagers. As a tavern keeper, he met and talked with the travellers who put up at his hostelry, thus maintaining a contact with the outside world vouchsafed to no others in the town."

As a leader of the community, Ebenezer did not like the news in September of 1775, when British troops marched out of Boston to seize several cannon and a quantity of powder belonging to the citizenry. He organized a group to stockpile arms for the conflict he was sure would come, and when word arrived of the shots fired at Lexington and Concord, Ebenezer personally equipped a cavalry company and trained it on the Sturbridge village green. Crafts and his troops were eventually used to help relieve the siege of Boston. He returned home a colonel, but, like several patriots of the time, Crafts paid a high price for his

Johnny Tremain was here,

as well as George Washington, who paid a brief visit in 1771. The décor of the sitting room, left, remains unchanged, as do the holiday traditions. Christmas finds the inn decorated in a riot of pine boughs and colored lights. Cooks labor for weeks to create such treats as this 800-pound gingerbread house, above, completely decorated with edible furnishings.

Home for the holidays.

The gingerbread village and holiday lights enhance the inn's traditional Christmas atmosphere. Reservations for the festivities must be made far in advance. Private dining facilities include the Pumpkin Room at left, so named for its pumpkin pine walls.

A clear fire, a clean hearth . . .

In Ebenezer Crafts's day, meals were cooked in this enormous walk-in fireplace. The eight full-time cooks and five bakers employed by the inn today require a larger, more modern kitchen.

revolutionary ardor. He lost the tavern during the postwar inflation fired by the flood of worthless Continental paper currency. The old warrior left Sturbridge, but he wasn't finished by any means. He moved up to Vermont, founded the community of Craftsbury and was its leading citizen until his death in 1810.

More than two hundred years after it was built, Ebenezer's fine old establishment still stands as the Publick House in historic Sturbridge. Its hallways and sloping, irregular floors, some of them made from red pine now rare in New England, bespeak its eighteenth-century heritage, while the air conditioning, the telephones in every room and the modern baths make it a very up-to-date facility. The twenty-one guest rooms are well designed and comfortable. With exposed oak beams and many old-fashioned decorating touches, such as a wooden ice bucket that doubles as a waste basket, flowered wallpaper, white organdy curtains and a tall chair with its own writing arm, a room in the Publick House combines the best in traditional and contemporary innkeeping. The public sitting rooms, with beautiful braided rugs and wide plank floors, feature a brace of cozy chairs comfortable enough to nap in. The taproom is a popular meeting spot, with a huge open fireplace decorated with a collection of copper kettles and pots. The inn's dining room, in the old barn, can accommodate as many as two hundred guests at a time, but the old timber stalls break up the room nicely and allow for considerable privacy. Chef Al Cournoyer runs a big operation, with eight full-time cooks and five bakers turning out house specialties.

Breakfast at the Publick House is famous throughout the state. The traditional farmer's breakfast is tailor-made for people with hearty appetites. It consists of hot mulled cider, red flannel hash with eggs, freshly baked New England breads, sweet pecan rolls, muffins, deep-dish apple pie and coffee.

As befits its name, the Publick House is always bustling, filled with people who have come from all over the world to visit the historic restoration at Old Sturbridge Village a few miles away. A massive enterprise encompassing some two hundred acres, Old Sturbridge Village is an authentic re-creation of New England rural life during the eighteenth and nineteenth centuries. Nearly forty buildings have been moved there from various New England towns, restored, and furnished in their original styles. Old Sturbridge includes a working farm, a general store, a tinsmith, a bank, a schoolhouse and a grist mill among many other exhibits, as well as private houses of every type, from simple country cottages to imposing formal residences.

The Publick House is a merry place, especially during the winter, when the management holds a series of weekend parties for the guests, with horse-drawn sleigh rides and gargantuan holiday meals. It goes all-out for Christmas, and keeps the traditional twelve days of the season with a riot of celebrations that conjure up holiday rites from pagan, English, Teutonic and Scandinavian observances. Students from nearby music schools serenade the tables with traditional Elizabethan airs. Each chef has his own project to prepare, and the whole kitchen staff gets together to make a gigantic Christmas cake from some three thousand gingerbread cookies, which weighs over eight hundred pounds when completed. The final holiday feast features a Boar's Head Procession, with a roast suckling pig, roast goose, platters of venison and plum pudding.

At that kind of party, old Ebenezer Crafts would have drained many a barrel.

Comfort the weary traveler.

Upstairs, the bedrooms feature organdies and four-posters in a colonial atmosphere with all of the modern amenities.

THE VICTORIAN

Whitinsville, Massachusetts

Some people are born to be innkeepers, although it may take them a while to find it out. Orin and Martha Flint joke now about how they finally discovered their calling. Orin was a graduate in electrical engineering, and Martha held a degree in business administration. "But when we decided to go out on our own," Martha explains, "we realized the only really useful things we knew about were cooking and cleaning. So we settled on opening a restaurant."

The Flints may not have gone to *l'Ecole hôtelière* in Switzerland, but they had an instinctive grasp of the essential elements of good innkeeping: concern for the kitchen and an eye for the day-to-day problems of maintenance and the comfort of their guests.

What they needed was a proper setting. After searching throughout much of New England, they found what they were looking for in a handsome nineteenth-century mansion in Whitinsville, Massachusetts. Built in 1871 for the owners of the local cotton mill, the house had fallen into some internal disrepair, but structurally it was as sound as the prosperous Victorian period it represented. While Orin did the repairs, Martha haunted the flea markets and nearby auctions looking for furnishings. Both did their work well. When the Victorian opened for business in 1975, it had been completely renovated. Its magnificent Italianate façade had been preserved while the inside of the house was completely but unobtrusively modernized. In the upstairs rooms, the air-conditioning units are all hidden in the closets. The original furnishings include a crystal dining room chandelier, and one of hammered copper in the main hall that has already caught the covetous eye of the Boston Museum of Fine Arts. To complement them Martha

Country splendor.

Built in 1871, the house is a mixture of Victorian styles. The smallest of the three dining rooms, above, was formerly the drawing room. With its blue moiré walls, it provides a luxurious setting for magnificent meals. Entrées are French, richly sauced and beautifully presented—blanquette de veau, filet de boeuf Madeira, frogs' legs, suprêmes de volaille, trout Niçoise—and crisp, tart salads refresh the palate afterwards; rich desserts then crown the meal.

has selected her purchases carefully, and almost all have gone up in value since she first bought them.

The spirit of the inn remains true to its Victorian heritage. The proportions of the white, mansard-roofed house are ample. Entering the front doors of etched glass, guests find a huge central hall as wide as the rooms on either side. To the right is the original book-lined library that runs the full length of the house, and now serves as the main dining room. Dinner guests can browse through the extensive collection of books gathered by a former owner of the house, Draper Whitin Allen. The books range in subject matter from ecclesiastical history to beekeeping, and they stand on the shelves where they always have, testimony to a more studious age and a grander conception of private space than most moderns can afford. Before them are drawn up tables resplendent with rich blue linen, sparkling glassware and candelabra.

To the left of the front hall is the original drawing room, which is now used for cocktails or for small special dinner parties. A splendid mahogany staircase takes overnight guests to their accommodations upstairs. The bedrooms on the second floor are as commodious as the public rooms below. One, the former master bedroom, has a separate dressing room with fitted drawers and mirrored closet doors. The baths combine the spaciousness of the Victorian period with the most modern of fixtures.

Throughout, the house is filled with the Victorian artifacts beloved

116

The little pleasures.

Laid out on a cutting board are the ingredients for the homemade dill bread served at every table. Scenic walking paths lined with wild flowers surround the mansion. Even in the bedrooms flowers are abundant, as the wallpaper and embroidered chair show in the room below.

Etched
glass
doors
welcome guests to the
Victorian. Orin found one
of them sitting in the barn.

by successful industrialists of a century ago. Renaissance paintings and Art Nouveau floral patterns seem perfectly at home against the woodwork of black walnut and mahogany.

The Victorian is a house of quiet pleasures. Golf and tennis are nearby, but most of the overnight guests come simply to relax, enjoy the sweeping views from their upstairs rooms and stroll through the extensive, wooded grounds.

Conservative columnist William F. Buckley was once accused of trying to turn back the clock. "I have no objection to turning back the clock," he replied, "if that is the right time." At the Victorian, the time is perpetually set in 1875, and what a splendid time that was.

From
another
era.
All six bedrooms are
spacious and comfortable,
but only the master
bedroom has this lavish
dressing room.

THE SPECTRUM
of American
artists & craftsmen

Brick magnificence.

When Jared Coffin's house was built, it was the most impressive building on Nantucket Island; it still is. The ship figurehead, inset, is mounted on the corner of a building on Main Street.

JARED COFFIN HOUSE

Nantucket Island, Massachusetts

Main Street Nantucket.

Brick sidewalks, simple signs, choice establishments and a wide thoroughfare make this one of the most unusual shopping streets in America.

Geologically speaking, Nantucket Island was formed from the debris of the last Ice Age, but the local Indian legend offers a much better story. Apparently, the giant spirit Moshup chucked his moccasins into the Atlantic Ocean one night, and they spilled out enough sand to form the island.

However it got there, the "little gray lady of the sea" has been an important part of American maritime history since the earliest days of the colonization of the New World. The English explorer Bartholomew Gosnold first espied the island in 1602. Two years later George Waymouth, noting the "whittish sandy cliffe" of Sankaty Head, charted the island's position. Nantucket was a whaling port for almost two centuries.

At first, seamen hunted right whales in the shallow coastal waters. Then in 1712, a ship under the command of Nantucket skipper Christopher Hussey was blown far out to sea by heavy winds and found itself in the middle of a school of sperm whales. The crew somehow managed to throw a harpoon into one of the sea-going behemoths, and deep-sea whaling began. By the early 1800s, deep-sea whaling was one of the principal industries in the Northeast, and Nantucket's whalers ranged every ocean on the globe in search of these giants of the sea.

Whaling was difficult, dangerous work. Just finding whales could require a voyage of up to five years. Once discovered, the whales were no easy catch for men in small boats on a swelling ocean. A sperm whale could crush one of the frail boats with its tail. A wounded blue whale with a harpoon in its side could churn through the water at twenty-five miles an hour, sending the men above on what became known as a "Nantucket sleigh ride."

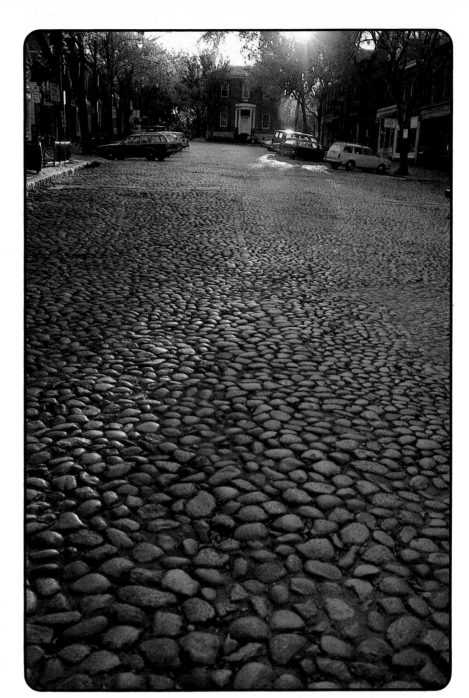

Another view

of Main Street, surfaced with stones brought to the island as ballast in ships.

The clock turned back.

Although automobiles are allowed, tourists often come to the island just to ride bicycles across the open moors to the sea.

For those who hung on and survived, however, there were rich profits to be made. For Jared Coffin, one of the island's most successful ship owners, there were enough for him to build, in 1845, the largest mansion on Nantucket. The usual building material at the time was wood. Coffin, however, wanted something more substantial to demonstrate his high position in the community, so he put up the first three-story house on the island built entirely of English brick, topped by an imposing roof of Welsh slate. The next year, his neighbors had reason to be grateful for his elevated tastes. A fire swept through the town, consuming most of the old wooden structures. But Jared's brick fortress not only survived the flames, it helped stem the spread of the fire and saved the rest of the community.

Through the years, the Jared Coffin House had several owners who altered its appearance with a series of unfortunate additions. But in

Restorative powers.

All of the restored rooms are meticulously maintained. The draperies, spread and canopy shown above are of matching crewel work; the carved four-poster and detail below are two more examples of the riches the inn contains.

125

The staircase

is just magnificent; it rises three floors to a cupola that looks out over the town and harbor.

1961, the Nantucket Historical Trust bought the place and restored it to its original grandeur. Now owned and operated by Philip Read, the Jared Coffin House is one of the most famous guest houses in New England.

Everything from the slender, graceful front hall stairway and the many black marble fireplaces throughout the house, to the thousands of yards of crewel work used to decorate three of the upstairs bedrooms is exactly as the doughty Jared Coffin would have wanted. The downstairs living room and library are furnished with Chippendale, Sheraton and American Federal pieces. These traditional American furnishings are complemented by evidences of the old China trade. There are several Oriental rugs along with many excellent examples of the best in lacquered cabinet work from nineteenth-century China and

Japan. The Coffin family crest and other memorabilia of the family are much in evidence. The library has a charming portrait of three of Jared's grandchildren, all done up in their Sunday best.

The spirit of Jared Coffin's prosperous maritime heritage is carried on throughout the main rooms. The taproom is furnished with old, oak captain's chairs, and guests in the restaurant will find themselves enjoying the seafood specialties of the house using pistol-handled silverware and dining off Spode and Lowestoft china. The most prized overnight accommodations are the ten bedrooms upstairs in the house itself, which have been decorated with exceptional care. Two of them, furnished with authentic Continental and Nantucket pieces, have marble fireplaces and are set off by exquisitely embroidered bedspreads and canopies done in fruits, flowers and nautical motifs. In addition to the accommodations in the main part of the building, there are rooms in the Eben Allen wing and in the Daniel Webster House a few steps across the patio, where the furnishings are a pleasant mixture of modern and colonial.

Nantucket is primarily a summer resort, and while the Jared Coffin House is a year-round facility, the local citizens feel that their island really comes into its own when the summer people are gone and the November mists begin to roll in over the moors. The inn, however, is particularly active during the Thanksgiving and Christmas seasons, as longtime customers return to celebrate these holidays in a traditional New England setting. At Christmastime, the Greek Revival structure

The dining room's bay window provides a serene setting for enjoying the inn's fine cuisine.

SILVERMINE TAVERN

Norwalk, Connecticut

Silvermine Tavern was not originally intended to be a country inn, but it is naturally such an inviting place that it turned into one almost by accident. The first structure in the cluster of buildings which now makes up the Silvermine Tavern complex was a sawmill, built by Sammy Ryder more than two hundred years ago to produce wooden knobs and spindles. At various times during its long life, it has been a country store, a gentleman's country estate and a town meeting hall. Ken Byard, a prominent furniture and art dealer from New York City, bought the place in the 1920s to make it over into an antiques store and gallery for his personal collection of farm implements, commercial tools, weather vanes and American primitive paintings. At first, he just put up a few friends for the night in the nearby guest house. Then customers and tourists stopped to ask for accommodations in the comfortable house overlooking a tumbling waterfall, and Byard gradually found himself running a full-fledged tavern and country inn.

For outdoor dining, he added a series of bricked terraces and a magnificent wooden deck built among a stand of trees overlooking the mill pond. Byard sold Silvermine in 1955, but his informal touch remains strongly in evidence. Most of the décor and art objects throughout the tavern are from his original collection.

The present innkeeper is Francis Whitman, Jr., who runs Silvermine with his father. Francis grew up with the business, baking dinner rolls when he was eight. He is a graduate of the famous Cornell University School of Hotel Management and has served a tour with a large hotel chain. Since coming home to Silvermine, he has found that innkeeping has its own special problems, and its own special rewards. The maintenance of a two centuries-old establishment is a never-ending

Nature's way.

The mill pond dam, above, provides a bucolic setting for leisurely fishing. Tall trees filter the strong sunlight above the outdoor dining deck, a striking feature of the inn and certainly inviting. Here the inn's food, good as it may be, is a minor part of the total experience.

Overleaf: In full view of the deck, one wall of the inn is adorned with toys and tools from a simpler era, a small part of the total collection.

Stated simply.

The folk art and antiques which are abundant at Silvermine have a powerful, primitive eloquence. The lady at the bar is the "Miss Abigail" referred to in the text. The bedrooms, like the one above, are comfortable and colonial.

proposition, and he claims, "The plumbers, electricians and carpenters practically live here."

But when the fireplaces in the main rooms are glowing and the guests are enjoying themselves, dining on such house specialities as baked rainbow trout and homemade honey buns, and the house mascots, a brace of glorious white swans, glide gently across the pond, it all seems worthwhile.

Under the Whitman family's direction, the Silvermine Tavern has burgeoned into a major restaurant in the area while still retaining its old country inn heritage. The heart of the establishment is the tavern itself, with its extensive dining area. The main dining room, highlighted by a large brick fireplace painted white, is a storehouse of Early American artifacts. One of the most striking items, found near the service bar, is "Miss Abigail," a re-creation of a colonial lady in a neat bonnet and a becoming long dress, who is the only woman allowed by Connecticut state law to stand within three feet of a bar. There are bedrooms upstairs in the tavern, and additional facilities in the Coach House and Old Mill. Before being converted into living space, the Old

Mill was operated as a waffle shop that became a favorite hangout for many of the artists and actors who lived in the area. Spencer Tracy and Katharine Hepburn ate there regularly, and Tracy holds the record for the most waffles ever consumed at a single sitting.

Another major attraction of Silvermine is the Country Store located just across the street from the tavern. The Country Store is both an emporium and an informal museum. It is a splendid evocation of the days when everybody in town stopped by the general store to do their shopping and to keep up with their neighbors. Today, the store sells old-fashioned candy and other New England food specialties, along with a line of Early American reproductions. For people just browsing, the checkerboard, set up right next to the mandatory pot-bellied stove, is always at the ready.

Just down the road from the tavern is one of the most unusual community associations in America, the Silvermine Guild of Artists. The Guild was started informally by the sculptor, Solon Hannibal Borglum. He organized the Knocker's Club, a group of local artists who gathered weekly to share a sociable drink and "knock" one another's work. Eventually, these meetings led to the creation of the Guild, a combination of studios, workshops, galleries and schools, where all the arts—including painting, sculpting, music and dance— are pursued in an atmosphere of mutual cooperation. The Guild now comprises the largest independent cultural center in the East, and is well worth a visit from anyone dropping by the Silvermine Tavern.

The Silvermine Tavern gets its name from an old legend. In the eighteenth century, one of the first settlers claimed to have a silver strike at the foot of nearby Comstock Hill. Prospectors flocked to the area, and the little byway called itself Silvermine before anyone discovered there was nothing there to mine. Since the stories of silver deposits were false, the town was eventually split up and divided among the neighboring communities of Wilton, New Canaan and Norwalk. But more than two hundred years later, the Silvermine Tavern remains the genuine article, a real treasure.

137

Back to basics.

Originally the local post office, Silvermine's Country Store is now a convivial meeting place. Browsing is welcomed, but buying things is even more fun. The colorful copies of early pressed glass displayed in the windows are beautifully made, sturdy and particularly useful.

GRISWOLD INN

Essex, Connecticut

No telephone

will ever ring in a guest's room at the Griswold—there aren't any, The two-hundred-year-old inn, above, stretches white and gleaming along the main street of Essex, an old seaport near the mouth of the Connecticut River. The inn is only one of many beautifully kept old buildings in the town, the house, inset, is another.

The Tap Room.

The Griswold's Tap Room, *overleaf,* displays the inn's amazing collection of marine art. Nameboards from sailing craft are placed between tiers of pictures.

William Winterer is a sailor who loves ships and the sea; so naturally he lives in Essex, which has been a sailor's haven for over two hundred years. The first warship of the Continental Navy, the *Oliver Cromwell,* was built and commissioned here in 1776. As time passed, large ships were no longer built in Essex, but yachtsmen and boat enthusiasts today still make the town a regular port of call. Winterer discovered Essex in 1957 when he was a cadet at the Coast Guard Academy in nearby New London. But there was another attraction for Bill Winterer besides a sailor's natural love for a safe harbor. It was the historic Griswold Inn that had first opened for business, promising "first class accommodations," the year the *Oliver Cromwell* was commissioned.

"I was in love with the old Griswold," Winterer recalls. "The Tap Room was the handsomest bar I had ever seen in America. Besides being a wonderful tavern, the Griswold had one of the finest collections of marine art in the nation and I fell under its spell. I had a fifteen-year courtship with the Griswold, and in 1972 I consummated it by giving up my career as an investment banker and buying the place to become an innkeeper."

Winterer also found he had purchased a good-sized hunk of local history. When the British seized Essex during the War of 1812, they made the Griswold their headquarters. As occupations go, it was a civilized affair. The British may have burnt all of the ships in the harbor, but they spared the town itself. As a gesture toward the local citizens, they kept the Tap Room open for business and instituted the custom of serving a huge English hunt breakfast every Sunday morning, a tradition that is still carried on today. When the British evacuated, they left the Griswold as neat as they had found it, and the English

On the waterfront.

A mural in the library, now one of the inn's dining rooms, shows Essex in the nineteenth century, when the Griswold still had its balcony.

A shrimp cocktail

to begin. Lunch at the Griswold has become an institution in Essex, with some tables set aside for regulars. The inn has long been a meeting place for social and political figures.

The Griswold Mall

across the street houses a nice collection of small shops amidst a pleasant park.

commander gave the lady of the house across the street his personal sword as a memento. After the war, many British returned as guests to the Griswold where they had once been conquerors.

When the inn was originally built it was the first three-story building in the state of Connecticut. If Sala Griswold were to come back today, he would recognize his old place immediately. Except for the removal of a second-floor gallery, the structure has remained virtually unchanged for two hundred years. The downstairs area is a rabbit warren of attractive public rooms. There is the Tap Room—dominated by a huge potbellied stove that is kept burning from autumn until early spring while an antique popcorn machine serves up quantities of hot buttered popcorn. The original parlor of the inn is now a book-lined dining room where guests can read through any of several thousands of old volumes on the shelves. The area between the main building and the annex is the Steamboat Room, fitted out to duplicate the dining room of one of the old river steamers that used to run from Hartford to New York. All of the eating facilities are open every day of the year except Christmas.

Interspersed throughout all of the downstairs is the famous marine

143

Gillette Castle,

built by Shakespearean actor William Gillette as his home at the turn of the century. Gillette bequeathed it to the state, together with its extensive grounds and miniature railroad network, for use as a public park.

Goodspeed Opera House

in nearby East Haddam, where many recent Broadway hits were first seen.

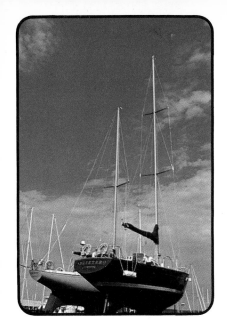

A sailing heritage.

Essex has long been known as a center of wood boat design, and as a harbor for the best boats built. The high masts of sailing craft out of the water for overhaul, above, and the busy marina, above right, testify to its importance as a pleasure port.

art collection as well as a library of firearms that informally traces the development of the handgun and rifle ever since the fifteenth century.

Upstairs is a score of small, comfortable overnight accommodations. As Winterer explains his philosophy of innkeeping, "Our rooms are centuries away from motel accommodations. Our brass beds and non-insistence on having a private bath in every room bear witness to that. Some of the floors upstairs have a port or starboard list that is over a century old, too, but that's the way we like the Griswold to be. Our goal is to provide the best of all possible worlds, old and new. We compromise by providing air conditioning and sprinkler systems and by accepting credit cards. But we don't tamper with things like fresh provisions and fine wine and whiskey. And good-sized portions. We cater to individuals, not groups. We have only twenty rooms, not two hundred, and neither television nor telephones are allowed to violate privacy. We simply do not allow them."

The Griswold Inn is filled with the sounds of live music every night of the week. There may be sea chanteys one night, a dixieland jazz band the next night and a banjo and tuba duet the night after that. No one knows for sure. The only guarantee at the Griswold is that it will never be rock 'n' roll.

In keeping with its status as one of the oldest institutions in Essex, the Griswold Inn plays an important role in civic and social life of the town. "We get involved in a great many community activities," says Winterer. "We put on an Oktoberfest every year and we help out with the annual Halloween parade that the fire department puts on. Across the road we have bought some property and put up the Griswold Mall, which is a garden area for our guests and for use by townspeople as well. During the last few years we have put on a community Christmas program. The New England Brass Quintet comes and plays for us, and we give out popcorn and soft drinks to the kids in the town and hot buttered rum to the adults. This isn't something we do just for business. We do it because we are part of this community. You know, in colonial times the local innkeeper was one of the most important men. His inn was an informal meeting place for everyone to meet and talk over their problems. The tradition of the American innkeeper is a valuable one and we are trying to maintain it."

145

THE INN
AT CASTLE HILL

Newport, Rhode Island

A place in the sun.

Both the richly furnished cocktail lounge and the expansive lawns provide a tranquil setting in the declining sun of a late summer day. Located on a thirty-two-acre estate, the inn, shown *overleaf*, commands the entrance to Newport Harbor.

Newport was once described as a place where people who don't have a care in the world go to get away from it all. Ever since the first "cottages" were erected in stone and marble more than a century ago by some of America's wealthiest families, Newport has been a national symbol for elegant high life. Players in crisp tennis whites still propel the ball over the manicured grass courts of Newport Casino, and every time some foreign yachting power launches an assault on the America's Cup, our defenses are rallied at Newport.

The Inn at Castle Hill is the perfect setting for this kind of elevated social scene. An imposing shingled mansion set on thirty-two acres on the Atlantic Ocean, it was built in 1874 by Alexander Agassiz. Son of the great Swiss-American naturalist, Louis Agassiz, Alexander was himself a noted scientist and is considered one of the founders of modern marine biology. Intended for use as both a summer home and a research laboratory, the house, with its jaunty silhouette, still proclaims its Swiss heritage. Many of the original appointments of the Agassiz home are still there, including the oak buffets placed throughout the house, and the huge safes for storing the family silverware. As befits a house that was largely constructed by ship's carpenters, the inn has a nautical flair, and guests in the ten upstairs rooms are treated to the feeling of traveling first class on a great ocean-going sailing vessel.

Under the direction of its present innkeeper, Paul McEnroe, the Inn at Castle Hill combines traditional New England hospitality with the most exacting of European-style service. In the several dining rooms, attentive waiters hover over chafing dishes, preparing classic meals with

The importance of being splendid.

Great food in magnificent settings is Castle Hill's forte. The Sunset Room at the left and the Agassiz Room on this page are two of the inn's dining rooms, where beautifully prepared platters are served with style. The broiled steak *garni*, opposite, illustrates the meticulous presentation common to all dishes.

Touches of class.

Overleaf: the Victorian roofline of the inn produces ununsual interior spaces, such as this third-floor bedroom. The delicate wicker furniture reminds us that the inn was once a summer cottage.

a dash of originality. The linen is of the finest quality, and each table is set with a distinctive china pattern. The paneled lounge welcomes yachtsmen and their crews with crisply prepared drinks served by stylishly gowned girls. Drinks are also sometimes served in the living hall, alive with mirrors and light, furnished with Victoriana. The proud maitre d' is also the sommelier. His cellar is as new as the management, but as extensive and selective as that of many restaurants with long-established reputations.

The Inn at Castle Hill is a natural gathering place for celebrities. For major occasions, such as the sailing of the Tall Ships in 1976, the inn opened its grounds to some five thousand people so they could watch the spectacle from the bluffs. When Hollywood needed a location to film the hit musical, *High Society,* it naturally chose Newport, and Grace Kelly stayed in one of the small guest houses at Castle Hill. More recently, Sir Laurence Olivier and the cast of *The Betsy* took time off for a clambake on Castle Hill grounds. The crewmen of America's

Cup teams, often dine at the inn, and Ted Turner celebrated mightily here when he led the recent defense in 1977.

Novelist Thornton Wilder was one of the inn's most frequent guests, and has the protagonist of his last novel, *Theophilus North,* spend some time in the pentagonal bedroom in a turret above the house. From "that magnificent room," Theophilus could see "the beacons of six light houses and hear the booming and chiming of as many sea buoys."

Perhaps the most celebrated guest of all, however, was the "ghost" of the Inn at Castle Hill. For many months the guests and staff were convinced the place was haunted by a troubled spirit who rattled around the house, turning on the washing machine in the middle of the night. Whoever it was, the spirit is now gone, and all is once again serene at Castle Hill. There were several possible explanations, but the one Paul McEnroe liked best maintained that it was the spirit of Agassiz's daughter-in-law, the last member of the family to own the house, who was just checking to see what the new management was doing to her old home. Content that the place was in good hands, she went back to her eternal rest.

Comfort with a view.

Most of the large, thoughtfully decorated bedrooms command views of the water. In some rooms the chestnut paneling is left natural, as below right; in others, it has been painted white. In many of the bedrooms, Ione Williams, from the Inn at Sawmill Farm, assisted innkeeper Paul McEnroe with the décor. The bath at the left is undoubtedly her touch.

THE INNS

Even an institution as timeless as a country inn is changeable. Ownerships are transferred, rooms are redecorated and chefs come and go. Undoubtedly some changes will be made in the establishments written about here. But their general character and appeal will most likely remain intact. In spite of changes, or perhaps because of them, most of these inns have already stood the test of time. Most changeable of all are rates, of course, but current rates are given so that readers will have a clear idea of the range of expense for each establishment. Reservations are necessary for accommodations at all the inns. Maps are provided only for those inns the editors felt particularly hard to locate. In regard to children and pets, it is best to ask each inn specifically about its policy.

ASTICOU INN, Northeast Harbor, Maine 04662; (207) 276-3344, George Stiles, Innkeeper. A 60-room resort hotel, with restaurant, in a sailing town on Mt. Desert Island. Private baths and shared baths. Open from mid-June to mid-September. Cranberry Lodge, across the street, is open the rest of the year. Rates at the Asticou range from $38 for a single room with bath to $90 for a cottage apartment, including dinner and breakfast. Breakfast, lunch and dinner served daily. No credit cards accepted. Swimming pool.

DIRECTIONS: Take Maine turnpike to Augusta, Me. 3 to Mt. Desert Island, then Me. 198 to Northeast Harbor. Turn left at junction of 198 and 3 just before the town. Inn is up the road on the right.

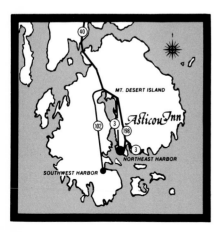

THE INN AT CASTLE HILL, Ocean Drive, Newport, Rhode Island 02840; (401) 849-3800, Paul McEnroe, Innkeeper. A 20-room inn, with restaurant, on a bluff at the entrance to Newport Harbor. Lodging available all year. Restaurant open from Memorial Day weekend to New Years's day. Lounge open on weekends throughout the year. In season, double occupancy rates, including Continental breakfast, are $26 for rooms with shared baths, $55 for rooms with private baths and harbor views. Two-room suite $70. Harbor House units $45. Beach houses with kitchen $235 to $260 per week. Lunch and dinner served daily. Master Charge and Visa credit cards accepted.

DIRECTIONS: From downtown Newport take Bellevue Avenue, which becomes Ten Mile Ocean Drive. Follow it around, watch for inn sign on left as drive turns back inland. Or take Thames Street to a right onto Ocean Drive; watch for inn sign on right, just past the coast guard station.

GRISWOLD INN, Main Street, Essex, Connecticut 06426; (203) 767-0991, William and Victoria Winterer, Innkeepers. A 20-room inn, with restaurant, in a sailing town on the Connecticut River. Private baths and shared baths. Single rates range from $19 to $28, with Continental breakfast. Open all year, exept Christmas day. Lunch and dinner served daily. Master Charge and American Express cards accepted. Sailing.

DIRECTIONS: I-95 to Conn. 9. Take Essex exit (3) onto Conn. 153, which becomes Main Street. Inn in town center.

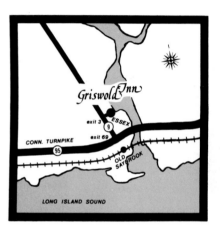

THE HOMESTEAD, Sugar Hill, New Hampshire 03585; (603) 823-5564, Esther Tefft Serafini, Innkeeper. A 17-room inn, with dining room, in the White Mountains. Private baths and shared baths. Open late May through March. Rates, usually including dinner and breakfast, are available on request. No credit cards accepted.

DIRECTIONS: Franconia exit from I-93, then drive through the town of Franconia to N.H. 117, which runs up to the left. The inn is two miles or so up the hill, on the left. From the west, I-91 to Wells River, then U.S. 302 east to N.H. 117. Inn is just beyond the town of Sugar Hill, on the right.

HOVEY MANOR, P.O. Box 60, North Hatley, Quebec, Canada JOB 2CO; (819)842-2421, Bob and Betty Brown, Innkeepers. A 34-room resort-inn, with restaurant, on a lake in ski country just north of Vermont. Private baths. Open all year. Room rates range from $30 to $44, double occupancy. Guests staying for six days or more qualify for a special rate that includes dinner and breakfast. Breakfast, lunch and dinner served daily. No credit cards accepted. Tennis courts.

DIRECTIONS: From I-91 in northern Vermont, pick up Canadian route 55. Take North Hatley exit (18), go east on route 108 about five miles. Turn right at the blinker to the inn. From Montreal turn south on 55 from Eastern Townships Autoroute and take same exit.

JARED COFFIN HOUSE, Broad Street, Nantucket Island, Massachusetts 02554; (617)288-2400, Philip and Margaret Read, Innkeepers. A 41-room inn, with restaurant, in Nantucket town. Private baths. Open all year. Room rates range from $16 to $20 for a single, from $35 to $50 for a double. Breakfast, lunch and dinner served daily. All major credit cards accepted. Confirmed reservations are imperative before making the trip to Nantucket.

DIRECTIONS: A ferry runs year-round from Woods Hole, Mass., to Nantucket. From Hyannis there is ferry service May through October. Call (617)548-5011 for ferry reservations, imperative for travelers taking automobiles to the island. The inn is straight up Broad Street, 300 yards from the ferry dock. Air service is available from Hyannis, Boston or New York.

LYME INN, on the Common, Lyme, New Hamsphire 03768; (603) 795-2222, Fred and Judy Siemons, Innkeepers. A 15-room inn with restaurant in a country town near Dartmouth College. Private baths and shared baths. Open all year. Rates for single rooms range from $14 to $20, from $20 to $30 for doubles. No children under eight. Breakfast and dinner served daily. No credit cards accepted.

DIRECTIONS: E. Thetford Vt. exit off I-91. Cross Connecticut River to Lyme. Town center is about two miles beyond crossing. Inn is at northeast end of Lyme Common. From Hanover, drive north on N.H. 10 approximately twelve miles to Lyme.

ISLAND HOUSE, Perkins Cove, Ogunquit, Maine 03907; (207) 646-8811, Paul and Marge Laurent, Innkeepers. A 6-room guest house by the ocean in a resort town on the Maine coast. Private baths and shared baths. Open from Memorial Day weekend through the end of September. Double occupancy rate is $37 a day, including breakfast, served every day except Sunday. No children under twelve, no pets. No credit cards accepted. Swimming.

DIRECTIONS: Take U.S. 1 to the center of Ogunquit, turn onto Shore Road through the town, and follow the signs to Perkins Cove. The Island House is the house farthest out, past the shops.

KILMUIR PLACE, Northeast Margaree, Cape Breton, Nova Scotia, Canada BOE 2HO; (902)248-2877, Ross and Isabel Taylor, Innkeepers. A 5-room country inn, with dining room, near a salmon river on the Cabot Trail. Shared baths. Open from June through mid-October. Rates are approximately $20 per person, dinner and breakfast included. No pets. No children under eight. No credit cards accepted. Fishing.

DIRECTIONS: From Canada 105, take Cabot Trail north at Nyanza to Northeast Margaree. From route 19, the coast road, take the Cabot Trail south from Margaree Forks.

MARSHLANDS INN, P.O. Box 1440, Sackville, New Brunswick, Canada EOA 300; (506) 536-0170, Herb and Alice Read, Innkeepers. A 16-room inn with restaurant near the Tantramar Marshes, close to the Bay of Fundy. Private baths and shared baths. Open most of the year; closed for at least two months including the Christmas season. Room rates range from $24 to $35, double occupancy. Breakfast, lunch and dinner served daily. Master Charge and Visa credit cards accepted.

DIRECTIONS: Trans-Canada Highway to Sackville, then N.B. 6 for a mile to center of town, where the inn is located.

THE OLD TAVERN, Grafton, Vermont 05146; (802) 843-2375, Lois Copping, Innkeeper. A 36-room inn, with restaurant, in a restored Vermont town. Private baths. Open all year except Christmas Day and the month of April. Room rates range from $30 to $45 a day, double occupancy. No children under 7. Breakfast, lunch and dinner served daily. No credit cards accepted. Tennis courts, swimming pool, skiing privileges.

DIRECTIONS: Exit 5 off I-91 at Bellows Falls to Vt. 121 west, which takes you through Saxton's River to Grafton. Inn is midway up village street.

PILGRIM'S INN, Deer Isle, Maine 04627; (207) 348-6615, George and Eleanor Pavloff, Innkeepers. A 9-room country inn, with dining room, on the Maine Coast. Shared baths. Open April through November. Inn may be rented from December through March by special arrangement. High season rates are $35 per person including dinner and breakfast. Weekly rates are $225. Master Charge and Visa credit cards accepted.

DIRECTIONS: North of Bucksport on U.S. 1, turn right onto Maine 15 and follow it to Deer Isle. In Deer Isle village, turn right onto the main street. Inn is one block down.

PUBLICK HOUSE, on the Common, Sturbridge, Massachusetts 01566; (617) 347-3313, Buddy Allen, Innkeeper. A 21-room inn, with restaurant, in a pre-

Revolutionary tavern near Sturbridge Village restoration. Private baths and shared baths. Open all year. Basic room rate is $32, double occupancy. Breakfast, lunch and dinner served daily. All major credit cards accepted.

DIRECTIONS: I-86 to Sturbridge exit, Mass. Turnpike to Exit 9. Inn is on Mass. 131, on Sturbridge Common.

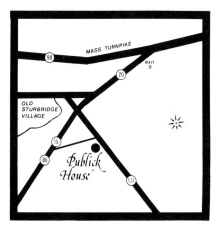

THE RED LION INN, Main Street, Stockbridge, Massachusetts 01262; (413) 298-5545, John and Jane Fitzpatrick, Innkeepers. A 105-room inn with restaurant in a beautiful southern Berkshire town. From December through June 30, when the inn has only 30 rooms available, all with private baths, double occupancy rates are $28 midweek and $32 on weekends. From July through October, the inn has 105 rooms available, some without baths. Midweek double occupancy rates are then $32 with bath, $26 without. Weekend rates are $48 with bath, $36 without. The inn is closed for two weeks in November. Breakfast, lunch and dinner served daily. Master Charge, American Express, Visa and Diner's Club credit cards accepted. Swimming pool.

DIRECTIONS: From the east, Mass. Turnpike to exit 2, Mass. 102 to Stockbridge, inn is at center of town; from the south, U.S. 7 to Stockbridge.

ROSSMOUNT INN, Rural Route 2, St. Andrews-by-the-Sea, New Brunswick, Canada EOG 2XO; (506) 529-3351. George and Marion Brewin, Innkeepers. A 20-room inn with restaurant, overlooking Passamoquoddy Bay. Private baths. Open from May through the end of September. Room rates range from $26 to $34 a day. Breakfast and dinner served daily. No credit cards accepted. Croquet, shuffleboard, swimming pool, jogging track, hiking trails.

DIRECTIONS: On N.B. 127, going towards St. Andrews, look for inn sign. A left turn and then another about a mile on will bring you to the inn, which is three miles north of St. Andrews on 127.

THE INN AT SAWMILL FARM, P.O. Box 8, West Dover, Vermont 05356; (802) 464-8131, Rodney and Ione Williams, Innkeepers. A 17-room country inn, with restaurant, built into a barn and several other buildings on an old farm near Mount Snow in southern Vermont. Private baths. Open all year except for a month in November and early December. Rates range from $80 to $90, double occupancy; suites with fireplace, $100; dinner and breakfast included. No children under eight. Restaurant serves breakfast and dinner only. No credit cards accepted. Swimming pool, tennis court.

DIRECTIONS: Vt. 100 north from Wilmington six miles to West Dover. Entrance to inn just north of West Dover town center.

SILVERMINE TAVERN, corner of Perry and Silvermine Avenues, Norwalk, Connecticut 06850; (203)847-4558. Francis Whitman, Sr. and Francis Whitman, Jr., Innkeepers. A 14-room inn, with restaurant, in a bucolic far suburb of New York City. Private baths. Open all year. Room rates range from $17 to $20 single, and from $29 to $32 double occupancy, including Continental breakfast. Lunch and dinner served daily. All major credit cards accepted.

DIRECTIONS: From Merritt Parkway exit 38, go east on Conn. 123 to a firehouse, then left onto Silvermine Avenue. From Meritt Parkway exits 39 and 40, N.Y. 7 south to light by Kelly Green garden center; take right onto Perry; street winds almost two miles to tavern.

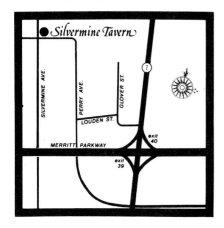

THE VICTORIAN, 583 Linwood Avenue, Whitinsville, Massachusetts 01588; (617) 234-2500, Orin and Martha Flint, Innkeepers. A 6-room country inn, with restaurant, midway between Worcester, Massachusetts and Providence, Rhode Island. Private baths and one shared bath. Open all year. Room rates range from $20 to $40, double occupancy, including Continental breakfast. Master

Charge and Visa credit cards accepted. Restaurant serves lunch and dinner daily, except Monday.

DIRECTIONS: From north on Mass. 146, take Purgatory Chasm exit. Drive into Whitinsville, take right at traffic light in town center onto Linwood Avenue. Inn is on left about a mile beyond center. Coming from south on 146, take Uxbridge exit, proceed about 2 miles beyond U bridge traffic lights on Mass. 122 to sign that says Whitinsville. Turn left; inn is on right beyond mill pond.

WHEATLEIGH, P.O. Box 824, Lenox, Massachusetts 01240; (413) 637-0610, A. David Weisgal and Florence Brooks-Dunay, Innkeepers. A 17-room inn, with restaurant, in a Palladian villa near Tanglewood. Private baths and shared baths. Open all year. Rates, including full breakfast, vary from $45 to $90, double occupancy, depending on the season and whether accommodations are for midweek or weekend. Breakfast, lunch and dinner served daily during summer season. American Express and Visa credit cards accepted. Swimming pool, tennis court.

DIRECTIONS: U.S. 7 to Stockbridge, straight ahead up the hill at junction with Stockbridge main street. Inn entrance on right about four miles on. Off Mass. 183, take West Hawthorne St., skirting Tanglewood grounds to inn entrance on left about a half mile down the road.

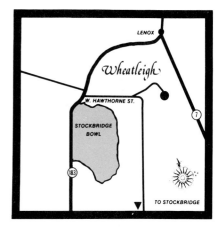

WINTER'S INN, P.O. Box 44, Kingfield, Maine 04947; (207)265-5421, Michael Thom, Innkeeper. A 9-room inn, with restaurant, in the mountains of western Maine. Private baths and shared baths. Open mid-December to mid-April and July 4 to mid-October. Summer room rates range from $8 per person for a dorm to $15 per person for a room with private bath. Non-holiday winter room rates range from $22 to $35 per person. A fifteen percent service charge is added to all bills. Breakfast, lunch and dinner served daily. American Express, Visa and Master Charge credit cards accepted. Swimming pool, tennis court.

DIRECTIONS: Me. Turnpike exit 12 to Me. 4 to Farmington, then Me. 27 to Kingfield. Turn left just beyond center of town, go down a block, then turn right up the hill behind the general store to the inn.

Photograph on page one taken at the Inn at Castle Hill by Lilo Raymond

Frontispiece photograph taken at the Publick House by George W. Gardner

Title page photograph taken at Wheatleigh by Lilo Raymond

A ROBERT REID, WIESER AND WIESER PRODUCTION CREATED FOR THE KNAPP PRESS, LOS ANGELES
WITH THE EDITORS OF ARCHITECTURAL DIGEST
EDITORIAL ASSOCIATES: GEORGE ALLEN AND TRACY ECCLESINE
DESIGNED AND PRODUCED BY THE VINJE, REID DESIGN STUDIO
COLOR SEPARATIONS BY OFFSET SEPARATIONS CORP, NEW YORK
TYPESET BY THE MONOTYPE COMPOSITION COMPANY, BALTIMORE
PRINTED AND BOUND BY W. A. KRUEGER